Open Borders
A Guide for Immigrating in the 21st Century

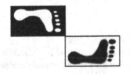

Andy Storm

Order this book online at www.trafford.com
or email orders@trafford.com

Most Trafford titles are also available at major online book retailers.

Note for Librarians: A cataloguing record for this book is available from Library
and Archives Canada at www.collectionscanada.ca/amicus/index-e.html

Printed in Victoria, BC, Canada.

ISBN: 978-1-4269-0552-0 (sc)

ISBN: 978-1-4269-0554-4 (e-book)

ISBN: 978-1-4269-0553-7 (dj)

Library of Congress Control Number: 2009931983
We at Trafford believe that it is the responsibility of us all, as both individuals
and corporations, to make choices that are environmentally and socially sound.
You, in turn, are supporting this responsible conduct each time you purchase
a Trafford book, or make use of our publishing services. To find out how you
are helping, please visit www.trafford.com/responsiblepublishing.html

Our mission is to efficiently provide the world's finest, most comprehensive book publishing
service, enabling every author to experience success. To find out how to publish your
book, your way, and have it available worldwide, visit us online at www.trafford.com

Trafford rev. 7/22/2009

Editing: Ellen D. Beck (Sea Breeze Productions)
Cover and interior graphical design: Andy Storm

 www.trafford.com

North America & international
toll-free: 1 888 232 4444 (USA & Canada)
phone: 250 383 6864 ♦ fax: 250 383 6804 ♦ email: info@trafford.com

The United Kingdom & Europe
phone: +44 (0)1865 487 395 ♦ local rate: 0845 230 9601
facsimile: +44 (0)1865 481 507 ♦ email: info.uk@trafford.com

To my wife and children for their
support, encouragement and understanding

Contents

Introduction

MY LOVE FOR storytelling has been a lifelong passion, but it wasn't until I reached my dream destination that I decided to pursue writing. A strong background in process development and constant exposure to international travel facilitated the collection of information and creation of the **guidelines** in this book. My experience in leading major projects gave me the confidence to undertake a publishing venture such as this.

Not long after my relocation, it became clear to me that others could benefit from everything I was learning. As time passed and I continued to gather information, a story began to unfold, the lessons learned and words of caution being at the forefront. Seven years later, with this impressive amount of information still vivid in my memory, my fingers started typing and wouldn't stop until everything had been shared. Sharing what I had learned about the immigration process fueled my motivation while developing this guide. The immigration process can be overwhelming and confusing, so my goal was to provide immigrants with a clear understanding of what to expect and then guide them along the way. I know that if I had

had the benefit of this resource when I was going through the process, my life would have been much easier!

While this guide is focused on helping you, the potential immigrant, navigate through the immigration process, it also offers information and advice to help you adapt to your new home.

Depending on where you are in the immigration process, you may want to flip through some sections at first and then read the rest of it over time. While this guide is not even close to being complete, considering the possibilities and situations you may encounter, it will identify many of the steps you will go through to integrate and become an active member of your new society.

Andy Storm
Spring 2009

Acknowledgements

THIS BOOK WOULD have never been written without my family agreeing to pursue the immigration adventure in the first place. Thank you! A special thank-you to my parents for their guidance and patience, and for sending me down the right path, laying the foundation of who I have become. A big thank-you to my grandparents as well, who took good care of me, resulting in my keeping all ten fingers intact so I could type this book!

Ellen D. Beck (Sea Breeze Productions) is right in saying "Behind every good book is a great editor!" Her determination to make the best out of my manuscript is reflected in this book. Ellen, I'm so lucky to have you as my editor. Thank you for agreeing to work on my book, for being so patient and methodical, and for pushing to get the best out of me. I also thank my good friend Ramona for reviewing, validating and providing helpful comments and suggestions on the financial sections of chapters X. 1 and XI. 2. These chapters would not have been part of the book otherwise.

Thank-you to the Internet and its infinite source of reference material, and to all my friends for being so patient with me every time I asked for direction, clarification, and fact-checking. Please know you are appreciated. I couldn't have gotten all the answers without you!

Open Borders

Part I - Planning for a New Life

CHAPTER I.

INQUIRIES, CONCLUSIONS, DECISIONS

I. 1   Dream Destination

GLOBALIZATION HAS PROMPTED people to imagine living outside their country's borders. The widespread use of English as the de facto language for business communication between nations has facilitated cross-border dialogue and ultimately tapping into human resource pools from abroad. The global economical situation has created new opportunities for citizens of countries where freedom of movement was previously restricted. In an effort to increase productivity while reducing production costs, many developed countries have opened their doors to immigration and embraced enthusiastic workers who aspire to wealth and a better life.

It all starts with a dream. You've heard that people can make a better living in another country and want the same for your family. The idea of moving abroad is appealing and intriguing. You start asking questions. Although you soon realize it's not easy, you still want to do it. Determination drives you to the next level and makes a goal out of what was initially just a thought. You fight for your dream. You talk to family and friends and try to convince them it's a good idea. Soon the desire becomes so strong that you start rejecting all discouraging remarks. You only want to hear about how good life is elsewhere.

But wait a minute! Where will you go? Somewhere far away? Somewhere cold or hot? You've heard of one particular place that has many things you like. Of course, there are other things about this place you dislike, but the wellbeing that awaits you there more than compensates for this. What you have learned so far about this place will help you set expectations and goals.

I. 2   Gathering Information

Before you make your decision, it's important to get a clear picture of what you will be facing when you immigrate. Knowing as much as possible about your adopted country beforehand will allow you to assimilate much easier once you've emigrated. Get all the information you can about the immigration process—what needs to be done; how long it takes; how much money is required; how to get a job, etc. Start with the Consulate/Embassy then the Internet, newspapers, friends and even travel consultants. Learn about the history of your chosen country, its government and the political and economic situation. Start reading newspapers from that country and learning about it as though it were already your home country. If you already have friends living in your dream country, they will be a valuable source of information. Ask them about the culture and social life, schools, childcare, medical system, insurance, taxes, rent, food, and so on. Find out about the customs, statutory holidays, and national celebrations.

Your friends or the Ministry of Labor (or the equivalent body) can explain the labor laws, which vary from country to country. How many hours per week are considered full-time employment? How will you be compensated for working over-time, night shifts or weekends? What is the normal vacation entitlement? In Spain, a typical workday is from 8 AM to 8 PM with a three-hour break between 2 PM and 5 PM. (Would it bother you to have such a work schedule every day?) Some countries like France have a workweek consisting of 35 hours (http://www.travail-solidarite.gouv.fr/informations-pratiques/fiches-pratiques/duree-du-travail/duree-legale-du-travail.html) and an annual vacation entitlement of 30 days (http://www.travail-solidarite.gouv.fr/foire-aux-questions/conges-payes.html). What you work in excess of that is considered overtime and compensated as such. Other countries have a 40-hour work week with an annual vacation entitlement of 10 days for new employees. It may be that your family life or certain medical conditions do not allow you to work 40-hour weeks with a minimum vacation entitlement or unpaid time off for sickness. Being well-informed will help you avoid unpleasant surprises later.

Below are two articles showing how countries stack up in terms of vacation entitlement:

www.canadaone.com/ezine/july07/vacation.html
http://www.cbc.ca/news/interactives/map-vacation-days/

When you immigrate to another country, you leave your life and your history behind—your home, job, business and non-business relationships, etc. You won't have your friends and family around you or be able to attend birthday parties, Friday night beer bashes or weekend parties. You have a mission: to live a better life in a new country. And that means starting all over again. Are you ready for this? It's a little like arriving from outer space and landing on a new planet you know very little about. (And whatever you do know probably came from books or talking to people who don't have firsthand experience with that place.) When you arrive in your new country, you are called a "landed immigrant" for good reason: you are nothing more than that. You will have to re-establish a brand new identity, starting from nothing. You will have to earn people's trust and prove things beyond your imagination. Why is it like this? I asked myself this same question until one day I realized the people in my adoptive country didn't know who I was or anything about me. Plus, I didn't speak their language very well. Since you probably won't have friends who can help you, you'll likely have to rely on your own devices to remedy this situation.

As I mentioned, when you move abroad, you give up a key element in your life: your network of friends and business associates. At your new destination, these people do not yet exist. Finding a job will be the fastest and healthiest way to integrate into your new society, as your co-workers can form part of your new social circle. But this may not be easy. Depending on your expectations, it may take you quite a while to find a company you like. In some countries, the cost of living is so high many people accept low-paying jobs just to get things started. For example, it could cost as much as $40,000 a year to support a family of three, depending on your lifestyle. (I suggest you refrain from bringing your family over until you've at least arranged for the bare necessities of life.) This means that the minimum income you need to earn per month (after taxes) is $3,333. If it takes you, say, three months to find work, you will have already spent about $9,999. For some people this amounts to their life savings. When you do find a company you'd like to work for, you will have to convince your employer that you are not only the perfect person for the job but also trustworthy and hardworking. (To prove yourself, you may have to go above and beyond the initially negotiated boundaries.) Unfortunately, as a rookie member of the workforce, you may not have the experience necessary to be accepted for the job you want.

I. 3   The Decision of a Lifetime

After working so diligently to put all the bits and pieces together, you start analyzing the pros and cons. You are a little confused and even scared. The magnitude of this project frightens you. This is not like any other project you've been involved with. This is "The Project." Will you be able to pull it off?

If this is the first time you have engaged in such a complex endeavor, it is understandable that you feel overwhelmed. A decision to start a new life in another country, where the grass is greener, the sun is brighter and rivers of milk and honey are flowing, should never be taken lightly!

If you have a family, the decision to immigrate will affect not only your future but that of your spouse and your children. If moving to another country was your idea, the people who depend on you may not like it. Like you, it may be difficult for them to leave behind friends, family or job. Generally speaking, people resist change (even if it's positive) so it's important to explain everything in detail and encourage dialogue. Your family members may not view things from the same perspective as you do. For them, the idea may not be appealing. Don't expect any sort of agreement before the message is well understood, questions are asked, answers provided and plans are adjusted and fine-tuned. Hopefully, they will support you in this initiative, as their support will be crucial once you get to your new destination.

Be open to change yourself. Even if you planned it all and the picture is clear in your mind, remember that what you view as logical may not be the same for the others. Like everything else, there are many ways to accomplish a goal. In this case, there are no set rules to immigration, other than the paperwork imposed by the Consulate or Embassy. It is up to you and your family to establish your own rules and the path ahead of you.

For example, let's say you have decided the best time to relocate would be this coming summer because you're tired of your current job and it appears there will be opportunities in dreamland next year. You know the immigration process will take about one year. Some other friends are also planning the same move and you don't want to go alone. As far as you are concerned, you can leave your job and move in one year. When you break the news to your spouse, you find out that a good friend has decided to get married next year. He or she does not want to miss the wedding and move to another country, far away from family and friends. This is a difficult situation to deal with, and you will have to use all your skills to work out the situation. In some instances, this could mean the end of the adventure.

The decision process is a difficult but important step. Once you decide to go ahead and invest in your adventure, don't look back as it will be increasingly difficult to stop the process. Move forward only if you are firmly committed to making this change in your life—barring unforeseen circumstances beyond your control that force you to rethink the whole process or reverse your decision.

CHAPTER II.

GETTING READY

II. 1   The Immigration Process

MOVING TO ANOTHER country is different from visiting it as a tourist. In order to control immigration and prevent an exodus of people from one place to another, governments have instituted clear rules and regulations. To find out specifically what you need to do, check with the Consulate or Embassy of the country you have chosen as your destination. In most cases, your starting point will be to obtain an Immigration Package. This may contain forms for you and your family to fill out. In some cases, you may have to undergo a police background check and obtain a certificate stating the existence or non-existence of a file on you for past civil or criminal charges. You will likely be required to prove that you can support yourself and your family once you move. The Canadian immigration system, for example, operates on a point system. You would be granted points for your education level, marriage status, family members already living in Canada, standing work offer, age, and how well you write and speak English and/or French. For more information on the Canadian immigration system, visit the Citizenship and Immigration Canada website http://www.cic.gc.ca/. You can also review the rules and regulation for immigrating to United States of America at http://www.uscis.gov/ . I'm including details about these two countries because they have attracted a considerable number of people from all over the world.

Completing all the steps in the immigration process will require time, money, dedication and perseverance. Be aware that all the documents in the immigration file must be in the official language of your destination country. In other words, an authorized translator—or in some cases a public notary—will need to authenticate the translation of all your supporting documents. To save money, I suggest you take the paperwork to an office that will do both the translation and the authentication. If you delegate someone to perform this task for you, choose a person or agency you can trust to handle your personal information. Of course, you must compensate them for their services.

In the documentation for your immigration file, you will need to prove that you are able to financially support your family (your spouse and children) upon landing in your adopted country. The requirements differ from country to country, but you will need to show proof that the funds exist in a bank or property. This may be in the form of a bank account statement or property deed early in the process and a bank draft or traveler's check towards the end. One notable exception to this rule is if you are immigrating for work purposes and the company employing you abroad has provided supporting documentation to prove your employment, thereby verifying that you have a means of supporting your family in the new country.

If you have gotten this far and money has become a problem, don't get discouraged. Don't let lack of money stand in the way of your goal. Consult with other people who have gone through the immigration process. Ask them how they dealt with this. Did they borrow money from friends and family? Did they change jobs or take on a second one? If you still don't have enough money after you have considered all the possibilities, you may have to adjust your timeline. Giving yourself more time may prove to be in your best interests in the long run, as the immigration process can take months or years. During this time, you can join online discussion groups or forums where people already living where you are planning to live have posted notes, or meet with consultants who provide immigration services. They may have solutions for some of the challenges you are facing.

II. 2   The Application Process

Once you have decided to go ahead and build your immigration file, follow the instructions, collect all the details and fill out the application. You will most likely be asked to indicate the destination city on the application. There are several factors to consider when selecting the destination city, namely the quality of education, crime rate information, transit/bus system, friends already living there, year-round weather, economic situation, etc. It is too early to consider elements such as the city area, grocery store locations and the routing to your workplace, but these will become important once you start making housing, school and job arrangements.

Once you've submitted your application, be prepared to wait—the process can take from six to twelve months or longer. During this time, I suggest that you:

0   Decide what you need to take with you and which items you will sell or give away;
0   Learn all you can about your destination country;

0   Think about your move. This is a big task and needs to be planned properly.

Check regularly on the status of your application—I recommend every two months. While waiting for a response, it's important to follow up with the Immigration office to ensure the process has not been delayed because of missing information. Because the immigration process involves communication via mail, it is important that you maintain the same address as the one recorded on your application. To make sure you're receiving all your mail, ask a friend to send you a letter, or send one to yourself. Pay attention to how long it takes to get to you. Check your mailbox daily.

When your application is complete, the Immigration office will inform you by mail if you are accepted or not. If you are accepted, you may be invited to the Consular office for an interview. Later, you will receive your Immigration visa and other supporting documentation. (In some instances, you may be required to send your passport via mail in order to receive your visa.) Take good care of the official immigration documents you receive from the Consular office! You've put a lot of effort into getting them, and you will need them to move forward.

Here is a rough idea of the steps and the timeline involved from when you file your application with the immigration office until you receive your final instructions:

1.   Confirmation of receipt of the application and information on the next steps (3 to 6 months)
2.   Acceptance notice and invitation to attend an interview. Possible request for additional information. Request for medical (and language proficiency) examination if the interview yields positive results (6 to 12 months)
3.   Final instructions. Receiving the visa (9 to 24 months)

II. 3   Making Plans

When you have received your acceptance notice and are waiting for the visa and final instructions from the Immigration office, you can start planning your move! You will have a limited amount of time (between 2 and 4 months) to complete all your preparation activities, both at the point of origin and at your destination, so you must be organized!

First, I suggest you consider some of the issues involved in a long-distance relocation, such as vacating your current residence, travel planning, selling assets you cannot take with you, learning about the health and education system in your chosen city, and looking for a job. If possible, identify the area or areas where you would like to establish residence in your destination city and determine the availability of housing (rent/lease or buy). Notify your municipal and other governmental agencies of your plans to permanently relocate to ensure you are removed from the electors' list and taxes registry (property and income).

To Sell or Not to Sell

If you own your current residence, you may decide to either rent it or sell it. If you choose to make it available for rent, consider visiting a public notary with your trustee of choice to give him/her executive power over your property. If you are moving far away, you will likely not have the time or money to fly back if your presence is needed to address issues concerning the property. The trustee will have the authority to act as your property manager and to maintain and rent the premises on your behalf. If you do not own your current residence, inform the property owner of your plans to leave. You may have to give notice, vacate or follow other instructions pursuant to your lease. Check this information carefully, as it may impact your plans. You don't want any unexpected surprises!

Think about the personal belongings you want to sell and which household items you want to bring with you. You will have to make arrangements to ship very heavy or very large items. No matter which transportation method you select, there will be limits and restrictions on the weight, size and type of items you can take with you. Contact the airline, rail or bus line, shipping company or your travel agent to find out what it will cost to ship your belongings to your destination city. This will give you a better idea of what you must sell, give away or ship (via air, land or sea.) If it costs you $100 to ship a TV, for example, find out how much it costs to buy a new or used one at your destination. If it costs you only $200 to buy a new TV and you can sell your old one for $100, consider selling it rather than shipping it. That way, there's one less item to worry about and you'll end up with a new TV for the same cost ($100). Also, the voltage and plug type at your new destination will likely not be compatible with your TV.

The items that you decide to take with you will be viewed as "imports" in your new country. Most countries have rules and regulations in effect for these types of items. The restrictions apply to a variety of goods including chemicals, food, animals, souvenirs, medication, plants, and textiles. You will need to find out which items are restricted and which ones are absolutely prohibited. A restriction indicates that you need written permission to import the goods, whereas an absolute prohibition indicates that you are not allowed to import the goods under any circumstances. If you bring restricted items into your new country, you could end up spending a lot of time at Customs, possibly paying fines, or even being prosecuted under the law. Below are links to websites that identify items restricted by U.S., Australia and Canada:

http://www.cbp.gov/xp/cgov/travel/vacation/kbyg/prohibited_restricted.xml
http://www.customs.gov.au/site/page.cfm?u=4369

http://www.cbsa-asfc.gc.ca/publications/pub/rc4151-eng.html

The Job Market

You will need a job to support you and your family. At this stage in the process, I recommend you do some preliminary research on the job market in your destination city:

1. Identify the industry and type of job you are interested in and then look for established companies in the area that meet your criteria.
2. Identify preferred employers. To determine how these companies rank against each other, search online by "company ranking" or contact independent consulting firms that establish company rankings at the national or regional level.
3. Identify employment agencies in the area and learn about their requirements for accepting applications.

Finding employment in a new city is not the same as doing so in your country of origin, where you have lived all your life, know the culture and have a network of friends. Networking is always a key element in getting a good job, so building a new network of friends and professionals is crucial. Language also plays an important role. If possible, learn to speak the local language; it will make your life much easier!

The Housing Market

Your first step in finding a place to live is to become familiar with the neighborhoods of your destination city and identify the ones that suit your needs and lifestyle. Living close to downtown will give you easy access to popular clubs and restaurants but is also noisier than living at the edge of the city or in the suburbs. If you prefer a quiet environment, look for areas surrounded by lots of green space and parks. Use one of the satellite map providers on the Internet to remotely survey the city online and select areas based on your preferences. If privacy is also important to you, look for neighborhoods in which the houses or apartment buildings aren't grouped closely together. While you are conducting your survey, be on the lookout for sports centers and fields for football, soccer, baseball, tennis, etc. These are easily spotted on an aerial map, often adjacent to sport centers. Also note the proximity to shopping malls, supermarkets and grocery stores, schools, businesses, parks and medical centers.

Once you have identified the areas in which you would like to live, check to see how they rank. You can do this by talking to friends already living in that city and accessing online forums or discussion groups. The local police or municipal office will have rankings and/or statistics on the crime rate in their respective neighborhoods. Find the address and contact information for the local police department by searching online for "police <city name>." Find the address and contact information for the city administration office by searching online for "city of <city name>" or "<city name> city." Then call or send an email to ask for the information.

Once you have created a shortlist of your preferred areas, search for availability of housing in these areas, as well as details on how to rent, lease or purchase. If, for example, you want to rent a house on Sunshine avenue in Boston, search online using the keywords "rent sunshine ave boston." If you don't get lucky the first time, don't despair—you'll have plenty of leads to start a new, more relevant search. Another way to approach the search is to seek out real estate agents. Try "real estate <city name>" or "rent <city name>" (replace "rent" with "buy" or "lease" as appropriate).

After doing all of this, make no decisions until you have an opportunity to personally visit the houses or apartments you have selected. At this stage, you are just investigating your options and building a list that will hopefully speed up your search for a residence once you have made the move.

The Education System

If you have children, the education system at your new destination will be of prime importance to you. You may be required to send your child to a school in your neighborhood. Areas may also be organized in specific districts that include several neighborhoods. Check to see if any of the above applies to you. If you have a preference for a certain school based on academic achievement rankings, language or religion, you may have to reside close to that particular school.

Healthcare and Insurance

Inquire about health insurance and family doctors at your new destination. Familiarize yourself with the healthcare system. How will you be paying for health services for your family? Will you be required to purchase independent health insurance, or is health insurance state-subsidized, employer-sponsored or a combination of the two? The more you know, the better prepared you will be when it's time to set up health coverage at your destination.

At this point, you should have an idea where you will live, where your children will go to school and where your workplace might be located, and be ready to take the next step once the Consulate gives you the green light.

II. 4   Planning the Move

After a long wait, you finally receive your immigration visa and are given a deadline for entering your destination country! As previously mentioned, you will have a limited amount of time (between 2 and 4 months) to complete your preparation at both ends. If you miss the deadline stipulated in the entry visa, you could end up back at square one. In most cases, you would then have to reapply, wait the same amount of time and pay the same amount of money. You want to avoid this at all costs!

Finding Accommodation

Your first step should be to look into renting or leasing accommodation at your destination for at least six months. (If the minimum lease term is twelve months, don't worry. You can use this time to research better housing or investigate your other options.) The Ministry of Immigration will often provide a list of support groups and community groups to immigrants as part of their Integration Support Services. The fastest way to find out what these support groups can do for you is to look them up on the Internet and then speak to one of their representatives.

When arranging for housing in your destination city, I also recommend that you:

  0   Identify the schools in the destination city;
  0   Learn about the community and the services available;
  0   Visit the city's web page to determine its short- and long-term initiatives. This is a good indicator of the health of the local economy;

0   If you haven't already done so, contact the local police and find out about the crime rate;

0   Know where the medical services centers are located. This is especially true if you have one or more children. The last thing you need in the middle of the night when your child has a fever is to start looking in the phone directory for an emergency medical service. Research the options and know in advance where they are located and how to contact them.

Some landlords may want to run a background check on you or check your credit history, which you may not have. Some may request cash only, 6 months' rent in advance, or both. If you find yourself in such a situation, ask your friends for help. If you don't know anyone at the destination, try to get in touch with a local community of members from your country. As a last resort, contact the Immigration office, as they might provide assistance for newcomers.

Your belongings

Start selling items you do not want to take with you to your new destination. I recommend you:

0   Post an ad online or in the Classified section of the newspaper;

0   Put up flyers or posters;

0   Talk to your friends—they can be very instrumental in spreading the word.

Make sure you tailor your ads to the appropriate audience. If you are selling a personal computer, for example, post a short ad with key specs on the news boards at a couple of universities in your city. If you are selling furniture, a specialty magazine would be your best bet. Once you have posted the ad, make sure you are available to take calls. Check your email often (if you used email as your preferred contact option).

Gradually set aside the items you want to take with you—do a little each day so you're not rushing at the last minute. Plan in advance and take everything you need. Be aware of the size and weight restrictions imposed by the airlines (and some bus lines).

Travel Arrangements

Check on flights, train or bus schedules. High and low season may affect the tickets price. Checking in advance will give you the advantage of choosing the departure date when tickets are more affordable. If you can, book your tickets in advance and, if possible, without making a payment. This gives you the flexibility to change the dates without incurring extra fees. Try to make the trip as simple as you can, minimizing the number of connections (and the number of times you must show your passport, visa, immigration papers, tickets, etc. and drag your luggage through stations or airports packed with people in a rush). A good travel agent will know what to do. If you do have connecting flights, make sure you have at least two hours between flights in case you are required to go through Customs and Immigration processing. (This will definitely be the case if you have one more flight to take after you have landed in your destination country.)

Having arranged the main part of your journey, you are now left with arranging the small but important task of getting from the airport/railway/bus station to your final destination. This can sometimes be difficult, so it is a good idea to find out what sort of transportation is available once you get off the plane/train/bus. If there is no one to investigate this for you at your destination, I suggest you search the Internet for taxicab companies servicing the destination and then call to inquire—just type in "airport taxi <destination city>." You will be surprised by how easy it is! If you have a lot of luggage, a mid-size taxicab may not be able to carry it all. A minivan may be the way to go. The size of cars and minivans varies from country to country—what you can fit in a minivan in North America will not fit in a minivan in Europe. If you have reservations at a hotel, use the hotel's shuttle service (most of the well known hotel chains offer this service). This will also save you money.

Money and Banking

Find out what payment methods are accepted by the landlord or hotel, taxi and food stores as well as the widely accepted payment methods in general. Determine approximately how much cash you'll need for the first few days and how you can get more later on. Make sure you have enough in the correct currency *before* you leave, and keep it safe.

Before you move, it's also a good idea to open a bank account in your destination city. Find out what banks have branches and offices in your chosen residential area and what types of accounts and services are available. For each type of bank account there will likely be monthly service fees, the amount of which depends on the balance in the account and the number of deposits and withdrawals.

Compare the options with other banks in the area. Some banks may offer features like grouping expenses by category, online reporting, and downloading your transaction history in a format compatible with widely used spreadsheet and financial applications. Many offer facilities for transferring money to accounts at other banks. Transferring money via e-mail is becoming more and more popular. This is where a person emails money to someone with an account at another financial institution in the same country.

Once you have opened a bank account, all the online payment services will be at your fingertips. This makes it easy to pay rent, insurance and various other bills including phone, Internet service, credit cards, electricity, water, etc. Most employers will also deposit your salary directly into a bank account.

Transportation

At some point after you arrive at your destination, you will want to rent or purchase a car so you can get around more easily. I discuss this in more detail in a later chapter, but for now I suggest you search out car rental companies in close proximity to your future residential area. If you would rather not drive, I recommend you purchase or rent a bicycle.

Although public transportation may be cost effective and environmentally friendly, some cities have complicated public transportation systems. Until you become familiar with the transit system, renting a car (provided you have a valid driver's license) or biking might be even better. Friends who live in the area can be of great help in situations like this. They could lend you their car or bicycle or provide you with a public transportation map so you can familiarize yourself with the schedules and routes.

CHAPTER III.

BEFORE DEPARTURE

III. 1 Saying Goodbye

LET ALL THE people you usually keep in touch with know that you will be leaving soon. Perhaps you could organize a party and invite them all to spend a few hours with you. Be sure to say goodbye to your coworkers. It is always good to maintain relationships with people you have known for a long time—you never know when you might need their help in the future. After you move, there may be times when you will feel lonely and down and want to talk to someone. Having friends wiling to help from a distance is invaluable. These people will also be your best source of news from the homeland.

Make sure the contact information you have for your friends is up-to-date. After you move, stay in touch with them. At first, your friends may be curious to hear your first impressions and opinions. Posting your stories and photos on a website is one way to share this information. There are plenty of Internet sites that provide this service for free, or you can build your own website. To keep the lines of communication open with your friends back home, consider creating an email account or Instant Messenger ID, both of which are free. Some Messenger accounts even allow off-line messages, file transfers and photo viewing. A digital camera is also a handy tool for sharing your experiences with friends and family.

III. 2   Last-Minute Details

Because you have been granted permanent residency in another country, it may be necessary for you to contact a ministry in your country of origin to provide details regarding your out-of-country residence. You may have to surrender your current identification documents (driver's license, health card, voting card, etc.) Some countries do not require you to go through any of this, in which case there's no need for you to do anything. I suggest you inquire, just to make sure everything is in order.

In case you decide to continue your education at a later date, I suggest you retain a copy of your education diplomas (and their translations). In order to gain admission to an education institution in your destination country, you may be required to provide proof of your previous degree(s). This is especially true for a Master's degree. Before you leave the country, visit your university or college to determine how a foreign institution should contact it.

Hand over the keys to your car and apartment or house (if they haven't already been sold). Give your moving company the go-ahead to ship the belongings you are not taking on the plane, train or bus, and arrange delivery at the new destination (timing and location).

Put your immigration documents in a safe but easily accessible place. Your passport and visa are the most valuable documents. With these in hand, you will be allowed to board all planes, transit through other countries and enter your destination country. Carry the phone numbers for the information desks of the station/airport and Consulate/Embassy of your origin country. Should something happen during your trip, these numbers will come in handy. If you know people in the cities you will be transiting through, get their phone numbers as well. (I once got stuck in an airport because of inclement weather and ended up spending the night on a bench along with hundreds of other passengers. This isn't fun, especially when you are jetlagged and have to look after kids and baggage.)

III. 3   Travel by Air, Step by Step

If you have never traveled on an international flight before, talk to someone who has. He or she will likely have a few tips to help make your journey easier. Here are a few things to keep in mind:

1.   When you arrive at the airport, head straight for the check-in counter of the airline you're flying with to obtain your boarding pass [http://en.wikipedia.org/wiki/Boarding_pass]. (Many airports offer automated check-in machines where you can do this yourself.) While checking in, you will be able to confirm the seat selection, make changes to it (if available at the time) and confirm how much luggage will be checked in. For check-in, you must show proof of your reservation (ticket or online booking confirmation) and answer a series of security-related questions. To confirm your identity and your entitlement to travel to your destination, an agent will ask to see your passport and visa. Be sure to answer all the agent's questions calmly and clearly.
2.   The suitcases you are taking on board will be weighed at this time. Make sure they comply with the weight

limits and size restrictions imposed by the airline. If they don't, you will be charged for the extra weight/ size! You are allowed to take a backpack or small piece of carry-on luggage with you on the plane. The agent may ask you to place this on the scale as well. The large luggage will then be labeled, pushed onto the conveyor belt and the boarding pass issued (not necessarily in that order). If you have connecting flights, you may receive more than one boarding pass. A label for each piece of luggage will be issued. Usually the agent will attach corresponding labels to your boarding pass. Don't forget to retrieve your passport, boarding pass and ticket. These are key documents, without which you cannot proceed any further. Ask the agent if the luggage will be transported all the way to your final destination. If you are required to pick up the luggage and check it in again while in transit, find out how to do this.

3. Check the details on the luggage labels attached to the boarding pass. Take note of the printed name, origin and destination airport codes and flight numbers. These will confirm if your luggage will go all the way through to your final destination. Place the boarding pass and these labels in a safe place. The labels contain the reference number for your luggage in case it gets misplaced or left behind at a terminal. (It is not unusual for luggage to be left behind at a terminal or mistakenly placed on the wrong aircraft.)

Your next step is to go through the security check.

When going through security, you will need to remove all metal items, belts and shoes and place them in a plastic bin on the conveyor belt. Remove all electronic devices from your pockets and bags and place them in a separate plastic bin. (Your electronic devices may be selected for a chemical elements check.) Place your plastic zip-lock bag containing liq-uids in a plastic bin as well. You will be asked to show your boarding pass before you are allowed to proceed.

When finished with security, collect all your belongings and proceed to the gate. The gate number is printed on your boarding pass along with the flight number, boarding time and seat number. In some countries there will be a border cross-ing point between security and the departure gate or between check-in and security, where you will be asked to show your passport once again. The border guard will check your pass-port and visa, and possibly ask you some questions before stamping your passport with the date and place of departure. At this point you have officially left that country and are in a duty-free zone. Do not spend too much time in the famous "duty-free" shops. Instead, head to the departure gate, which may be farther away than you realize. Time is precious in these moments.

At the boarding gate, pay attention to the announcements and follow the instructions pertaining to passengers who are traveling with children, the elderly, disabled, club members, first class passengers, etc. Priority is given to passengers in these categories. Also note instructions for boarding by seat numbers. Upon boarding, the agent will ask for your boarding pass and passport. He or she will scan the boarding pass and check the name and photo on the passport. As you board the plane, a flight attendant will check your boarding pass again and tell you where your seat is located. Place your carry-on bag in one of the overhead bins or under the seat in front of you. Know where your passport and boarding pass are located.

III. 4   Travel by Air, Connecting Flights

Check the boarding time of your connecting flight. This information will be printed on one of the boarding passes you received at check-in. (Sometimes the departure gate will also be noted, although this is very rare.) This will tell you how much time you have before your next flight. Since flights are sometimes delayed, it is a good idea to check the time before you reach the connection point. In preparation for landing there will be announcements about timing and in many cases connecting flights terminal and gate details.

Once you get off the plane, look for one of the large information screens located throughout all airports. (In some older airports they are located only in designated areas.) Look up your next flight number, departure terminal and gate number. If you cannot locate your flight number on the information screen, don't panic. Sometimes flight numbers differ from airline to airline and your flight may be operated by another airline. Look for a matching departure time and destination. It is highly unlikely that two planes will be departing for the same destination at the same time. Should your flight be delayed, be prepared to ask the information desk what options are available. If you miss your connection, you will need to contact a ticketing office, usually in the transit area, and make the necessary changes to your tickets. If you have friends waiting at your final destination, try to notify them via email or phone.

International airports often have more than one terminal, and each terminal can have many gates. Sometimes getting from one terminal to another involves taking a small train or shuttle. If you need to change terminals, find out how and where to catch the train or shuttle, how often it comes and how long it takes. On your way, make sure you stop by an information desk to double-check your flight and gate details. If you can't find the information desk, or there isn't enough time for this, look for people dressed in uniforms and ask them. If they don't know the answer, they will direct you to the nearest information desk.

Right before landing in your destination country, you will be handed a customs declaration form to fill in. By now you should be familiar with the restrictions on what you can and cannot bring into the country. If you have difficulty filling in the customs declaration form, ask a flight attendant to help you.

III. 5   Travel by Air, Reaching the Destination

If you have reached your destination country, this is when you will receive permanent resident status, which will enable you to reside for as long as you want in your new country!

When you leave the plane, look for a sign directing you to the Immigration processing desk. There will likely be special booths for processing newcomers. If this is not your final destination and the process is delayed, it may prevent you from catching your connecting flight. If your connecting flight departs less than ninety minutes after you land, notify a Customs and Immigration officer. He or she may be able to direct you to a shorter line or allow you to skip the line. Have all your documents ready, including passport, entry visa and any other documents that provide proof of your immigration acceptance. Be calm and listen carefully to the Immigration officer's instructions. The officer will ask a series of questions, which you must answer clearly and truthfully in the country's official language.

When you leave the Immigration desk, you will officially be a landed immigrant. Congratulations!

Now look for signs directing you to the luggage carousels. To find out which carousel contains the luggage from your flight, look for information panels in the luggage pickup area of the terminal, which display flight numbers and their corresponding carousels. If your luggage does not appear on the designated carousel after a long wait, look for the "Lost luggage" desk or office. A clerk will track your luggage using the information on the luggage labels attached to your boarding pass. He or she will inform you where your luggage is and approximately when you will be able to pick it up.

Part II - New Country, New Life

CHAPTER IV.

FIRST CONTACT

IV. 1   A Dream Comes True

EVEN IF YOU haven't arranged for someone to meet you at the airport, this will be an exciting time for you! Don't be surprised if shivers run down your spine, your heart starts to race or tears well up in your eyes. You might even feel like hugging someone! But brace yourself—your journey has just begun and you will be faced with more challenges. However, armed with the information from the previous chapters in this book, you will be well prepared for what lies ahead.

After collecting your luggage, board a car, shuttle or train and head to your temporary residence.

IV. 2   A New Home

You and your family will need to rest after your long journey. Hopefully, you will have already established a temporary residence to give you more time to familiarize yourselves with the city and its neighborhoods, and hired someone to help you

35

rent or lease the space on your behalf. Many landlords won't rent to you without actually meeting or talking to you. Others may agree to finalize arrangements via fax as long as you sign the agreement and send proper payment. If you were unable to find someone to help you secure a place to live, you may be able to contact an Immigration support group, if available at your destination. (Make sure you research this beforehand!)

If you were able to rent a place, you or the person assisting you should arrange beforehand to pick up the key to the building and the rental unit from the landlord. If not, you will likely end up staying at your friend's residence or in a hotel. (I don't recommend spending your first night on the streets of an unknown city.) If you do go to a hotel, make sure you have a valid credit card (in your name) and that the limit on the card is higher than the cost of the hotel. Most hotels accept VISA and MasterCard; some accept American Express. Many hotels will not accept cash. When checking into the hotel, also be prepared to present proper identification (your passport).

Whether you stay in a hotel or in a temporary residence (obviously, renting an apartment is more cost-effective than staying in a hotel, although the comfort may vary between the two), spend the first couple of days recovering from your trip. Give yourself time to think things through. You may feel somewhat disoriented, but this is normal; your mind and body are trying to readjust to your new environment. Focus your attention on the things you need to do—one at a time, in the order of importance. If you try to do everything all at once, you may become overwhelmed.

IV. 3 Getting Connected

When you left your country of origin, you disconnected yourself from the world around you. Now it's time to reconnect! It is really important to start this integration process as early as possible, so make it a priority. Resist the temptation to reconnect with things you are familiar with, i.e., TV, radio, friends. You don't have to completely sever your link to the past; just ensure you first establish a link to your new world.

In my view, there are three main common communication links you need most in today's modern world: TV, Internet and phone. Radio has certain significance as well, but I think you can live without it as long as you have TV and the Internet. As you well know, you can access radio programs over the Internet these days. The reality is that once you're in front of a computer, you have access to an entire world of news and entertainment. You may not even need a TV if you have the Internet, as you can get online access to TV programs, entertainment, communication and news.

With all this said, it seems clear that the first priority is the Internet. As you may be aware, there is a considerable lineup of options and providers. Your first step is to get a list of the reputable Internet Service Providers (ISPs) in your area, compare their rates for each of the services on their list, and make the best choice based on your budget and needs. The type of connection may determine which one you choose. Some are better than others, depending on what you are looking for. Pay attention to traffic limitation—that is, the amount of data transfer allowed in and out as part of the rate advertised by the provider (Note: this is different from the speed.) If you happen to see eye-popping low rates and very attractive promotions, you need to be vigilant and read the fine print. Also, pay close attention to time-limited promotions, deadlines and other hooks the marketing machine throws out there for you to grab. If there is a deadline on a promotion, do not dive right into it. Wait to see what happens after the promotion is over. There will likely be an extension. Do your calculations and find out how much it would cost you after a full year of usage. Why one full year? Because many providers offer three- or six-month promotions at reduced rates, after which time a full charge applies, which may or may not be lower than other providers' rates over the twelve-month period.

"Bundles" are the catch of the century. Do not commit to an Internet bundle if you don't need all the services in the bundle. Why? Because you will end up paying more than necessary. You might say, "But I'm getting all that extra stuff at a very good rate." Of course you are, but do you really need all those services? You likely won't have time to browse through, let alone watch, 150 TV channels. Don't pay for services you don't need. Spend your time and money wisely. Don't fall into a trap.

In terms of which is the better choice, technically speaking, between ADSL and cable, I would personally choose cable. This is just a personal preference, and you should do your own research to figure out which option works best for you. Going further, you can choose between a wired or wireless connection from the modem (ADSL or cable) to your computer via a router. If you choose wireless, make sure you know how to set the router up. Never use the default settings, as they usually aren't "encryption-enabled." If the encryption is not enabled, your neighbors or anyone else in the area will be able to use your Internet connection. This is not a safe practice and may even break the rules and conditions imposed by your ISP, which could lead to losing your service. I will not go into the details of setting up your computer, as there are numerous resources available for this, including the Internet, a local computer store, specialists or friends.

I highly recommend you get a telephone so that potential employers, agencies or other organization responding to your applications for a job can easily get in touch with you. (Online phone conversations via instant messenger are fine for keeping in touch with friends on an ad-hoc basis.) It is true you can use an IP phone or a computer, but not everyone is used to phoning other people from a computer. And IP phones aren't reliable (a power loss renders their adapters unusable).

Depending on the phone providers in your area, you may purchase "mobile" or "landline" phone service. No matter which phone you choose, I recommend an inexpensive one. And make sure you add the voice-messaging feature, or, in the case of a landline, purchase your own answering machine if it is more cost-effective. For example if the voice-messaging feature costs you $5 every month and an answering machine costs you $25, after five months you will have paid for the answering machine. Buying the device up front equates to five months of pre-paid service, but starting in month six, this feature will then be free. It's also important to check the "cost per minute." In some countries, landline communication providers offer free calls between users in the same area (also known as "free local calls.") In that case, choosing a mobile phone may not be the best deal. In other places, the landline usage is charged by the minute, which sets the stage for a competitive comparison between mobile and landline phone service. In North America, you are charged by the minute for using a mobile phone, even when you receive calls. This is called "air-time." Again, pay attention to bundles and promotions. Many sellers will let you have the mobile phone for free but require you to sign a contract for a certain number of months with a certain number of minutes per month. Be prepared to pay for between 300 and 800 minutes per month, or 10 to 26 minutes per day.

CHAPTER V.

HEALTH SERVICES

NOW IT'S TIME to focus your attention on four important things: *obtaining health insurance, finding employment,
schooling for your children* and *managing your expenses.*

To support the first two objectives you will need a means
of transportation. The options include renting a car, taking the
bus, driving a friend's car (provided you have a valid driver's
license), having a friend drive you around, riding a bicycle or
simply walking. If using the public transportation system will
meet your needs, I recommend you choose this option. It's
inexpensive and it won't take you long to familiarize yourself
with the routes and schedules. It is certainly the best option
for short trips, during rush hour periods (when buses ride in
their dedicated lanes), and in heavy traffic areas.

In order to obtain a bus pass, you will likely need a gov-
ernment-issued identification document. If you were issued
a resident card when you entered the country as part of your
immigration registration at the airport, or you received one
through the mail (if you provided the government with an address), you may already have an acceptable form of identifi-

cation. If not, you can purchase tickets for each trip. I suggest you locate an Information desk and get details on bus routes, schedules and where you can obtain tickets. (The subject of public transportation is discussed in greater detail in Chapter X.)

Health Insurance

Regardless of what country you live in, medical services must be paid for in one form or another, so obtaining health insurance should be very high on your "to do" list. You will need to enroll in a health insurance plan, obtain a health card and arrange for premiums to be paid. The immigration office should provide health insurance information and coverage details upon your arrival. If you are already employed, your employer may be able to tell you how to register with the local health care system and explain your options. If the company has a health insurance plan, your employer will follow the rules and regulations imposed by the government and may or may not pay for your health insurance. If you are self-employed, you will need some sort of coverage given the high cost of health care services in developed countries. In either case, find out what you need to do, what supporting documentation is required, what the conditions and wait times are before coverage is effective, the maximum period of time the company's coverage remains in effect if you lose your employment, etc.

Be sure to clarify what services are included in the basic insurance plan and whether or not your family members are covered too. (In some cases, your family members will not have medical coverage unless a policy is purchased specifically for them.) It is in your best interest to ask lots of questions and cover all the angles. Prescription drugs, vision care, dental care, chiropractors, physiotherapists, and coverage while traveling outside the area or country are just a few examples of services that may or may not be included. Be aware that basic insurance may not cover ambulance service. This means that if you are injured in a traffic accident, for example, you may end up paying for the ambulance trip to the hospital. If the insurance paid by your employer does not cover all the services you require, you will need to purchase a private insurance policy. It is also possible to be covered under two different health insurance plans, both of which are paid for by your employer. If your employer does not pay for any coverage, you will have to purchase coverage for both basic and additional services from a private insurance company.

You and your family will be insured as long as the premiums are being paid. In certain countries, your premiums will be paid by the government through taxes and it will appear as though you are getting free medical services. If you are in such a country, compare the taxes you are paying with those in other countries or systems where medical services do not appear to be "free."

Medical Centers and Treatment

Knowing where to go and who to call when you or a member of your family is not well is critical, so looking up the location of medical centers, walk-in clinics and emergency clinics in your area should be very high on your priority list. If you have small children, locate the medical centers and hospitals that are open 24/7 as well as "children's hospitals" that specialize in child treatment and intervention.

In a few countries, you and your family will have the option of enrolling with a general medical practitioner who becomes your "family doctor." Because this doctor learns your family's medical history and collects data related to their health over time, he or she is better able to prescribe certain treatments based on their individual needs. Most doctors don't make house calls. In emergency situations you'll probably have to rely on emergency clinics or hospitals. You should also be aware that some doctors may not accept new patients because they are overloaded.

In your new environment, your body may react differently to common viruses or other health threats. For example, you may catch a cold, which in your country of origin didn't affect your daily routine but in this new environment sends you to bed. To better prepare for this, find out what the most common and well-known treatments are for cold and flu. Most of them will be available over the counter (without prescription). Don't be surprised if the medication is different from what you are used to or that the medication you usually take is not even on the shelves. Rest assured that the medication will be effective in treating symptoms for viruses in that country. If what you are dealing with is not a regular flu or cold, it makes sense for you to see your doctor, who will recommend treatment and give you a prescription to take to a pharmacist. (In some countries, antibiotics can be purchased only with a prescription.)

CHAPTER VI.

EMPLOYMENT

IF YOU ALREADY have a job, your life just became a whole lot easier! If, on the other hand, you do not have a job, you will need a résumé, a target industry and range of positions you would be willing to accept. If you have connections, submit your résumé for their consideration. Start searching for employment agencies and enroll in their programs. Some employment agencies will call you for an interview and ask you to undergo some testing. Once registered in their database, you will be contacted should an opening match your abilities and goals.

Do not rely solely on employment agencies. Search on your own for availabilities at companies in your field of expertise. Review all the companies in the city and adjacent area then visit each of their web pages, check the job postings, and call them and ask for details on job openings or submit your résumé in person. Your main goal is to get a job as soon as possible.

Contact the immigration support service in your area and get as much information as you can from them. In some countries, the Immigration Assistance office allows you access to job banks and offer assistance in finding employment. Listen to the radio, read the newspapers, look for job fairs and postings. Searching for a job involves a lot of time and dedication. Treat this activity as a full-time job; dedicate at least eight hours of your day to it. On a lighter side, think of it as saving money—you don't have time to shop and buy things you don't really need!

For the purposes of this discussion, I will assume that you have not yet secured employment in your new home. In this chapter I will talk about the process and methods most organizations use to hire new employees, as well as the components of salary and benefit packages.

When organizations need to hire additional employees, they will choose ones who have knowledge in either their current line of business or in the new line of business they plan to launch. They will want to hire workers who are efficient, who require the least amount of training, and who have the knowledge and expertise to compete effectively in the marketplace. They may use their own human resources departments to handle the recruitment process, or they may hire an outside recruiting agency to interview the applicants, create a shortlist and make the final selection on their behalf.

Timing and having the right skills are important factors in finding work, but *networking* is also crucial. It is a lot easier to find a job in your preferred industry if you remain active within a network of professionals in that industry. This helps to keep you up-to-date with the latest developments and trends in that industry. Also, try to maintain the friendships you made at college or university. It won't take a lot of time or energy and may bode well for you in your job search. Another effective tool is word of mouth. If employers like what they see and hear, chances are you'll start receiving phone calls and invitations for further discussions and interviews.

VI. 1   The Hiring Process

The most important tool in the hiring process is your résumé. But even if you have prepared the best résumé possible, it may still end up in a pile among hundreds of others. If your résumé does end up in a pile, it means that too many others know what you know, which makes you no more special than anyone else. Every employer is looking for well-trained, skilled and trustworthy people, and unless you match their expectations you may not be chosen. As a newcomer, you bring education and experience gained abroad, which may not put you in a good position. (You can improve your résumé, cover letter and prepare for an interview by consulting the extensive Internet library on this subject.) So how do you get on the shortlist? You are the only one who can identify the gaps between what the employer is looking for and what you know. Your qualifications must somehow stand out. For example, if you have specialized in your field, you stand a better chance of being noticed. You also stand a better chance of getting an interview if someone you know recommends you for the job. This is where networking comes in.

Let's say I'm the one looking for a job and I'm prepared to do whatever it takes to find one. I prepare my résumé and distribute it, along with a cover letter, to various companies. While I wait for a response, I talk to my network of friends about my desire to get a job. Some of my friends either work for the companies I'm targeting or have friends who work for those companies. They are familiar with my background, qualifications, education and training and can speak to my character as well—something a résumé does not do. I quickly get called for an interview, which may not have happened if a friend hadn't put in a good word for me. It becomes obvious that I have a great advantage over any other outsider, *even if I don't have all the right qualifications for the job.*

People are always happy to be around other people they

know and like. Working with friends can make a day at work really fun. You can skip formalities, communicate more efficiently and reach consensus a lot faster. Knowing the backgrounds of the other people allows you to present ideas and concepts in a way they can easily understand. You have much in common and can draw from past experiences when formulating ideas. If you need clarification on a subject, you don't have to wait until the next business day to schedule an appointment or make a call. This creates a "team environment." A team is a self-sustaining entity that produces real results without repeated interference or guidance from a leader. Nowadays, more and more businesses are adopting the team concept. Why? Cohesive teams can take a business to the next level quickly.

In this example, the "friend" and "cohesive team" factors will likely outweigh some of the prerequisites for the job. As a result, I may be chosen over a very qualified and experienced individual simply because I meet the basic requirements, I have demonstrated a capacity and willingness to learn and grow, and I am a "team player." My addition to the team will not immediately improve its performance given I'm missing some of the requirements for the job, but having a solid knowledge base will enable me to come up to speed in a short time. Then the team will start performing at its best.

In conclusion, as long as you maintain a solid knowledge base in your desired field of expertise and spend time networking with people in that field, you will have a greater chance to obtain employment in that field (assuming your knowledge base matches the requirements for the job). Do not set unachievable and unrealistic goals for yourself. If it takes too long to find a job, it may be time to consider changing direction and looking for something that was second on your list. This does not mean you have to give up looking for your number one job. It just means that you might have to work at another job for a while and improve your skills so that you will be accepted in your preferred occupation.

VI. 2   Compensation Packages

Compensation includes not only regular remuneration but other benefits as well, such as medical and accident insurance, retirement saving plans and stock options. Some companies also offer permanent employees performance bonuses in addition to their yearly salary increases. A contractor is hired by a company for a specific job or project. A contractor may not be entitled to the same benefit package as a permanent employee. For the purposes of this discussion, I will focus on the compensation package as it applies to permanent employees. Keep in mind that certain components of the compensation package applicable to permanent employees may also apply to contract employees. You should also note that smaller companies tend not to include many benefits.

When it comes to negotiating your compensation package, there are several things to keep in mind:

Salary: This is the amount of money you will receive at regular time intervals in return for the work you perform. Ask if your benefits will be deducted from this amount. Calculate your annual salary *after taxes*. Find out how your salary will be paid out, i.e., before or after tax and deductions.

Paid vacation and statutory holidays: You should know what the vacation entitlement is for new employees and how it changes over time. For example, the policy may state that you start with three weeks and receive an additional week of vacation in your fifth year of employment with the company. Inquire if you will be entitled to paid statutory holidays and how many per year.

Hours of work: The regulated number of work hours per week varies from country to country. In most cases, there are 40 work hours every week, which comes down to about 8 hours per day. Some employers don't count the lunch hour as part of the 8 hours, so you would be required to spend about 9 hours in and/or around the workplace, for example from 8:00 AM to 5:00 PM. Other employers pay for half the lunch hour, in which case your workday would be 8 ½ hours, for example 8:00 AM to 4:30 PM. If you are offered a job that pays hourly, ask how many hours you are expected to work, how much time is allotted for lunch, how many breaks are allowed, and their length.

Overtime: This is one thing people often miss when negotiating their salary. Make sure to ask about the company's policy on overtime. Some companies do not consider time worked over regular hours to be overtime. Make sure you are not expected to stay in the office for several hours after the regular work day ends. Having to work constantly more than the regulated amount of hours per week will make it difficult to balance your work and personal life. Some companies pay 1.5 times the hourly rate for overtime during the week and 2.0 times the hourly rate on weekends. Some companies encourage employees to take time off in lieu of hours worked past regulated work hours. This means you are given one hour of time off for every hour worked over regular hours. Some companies offer variations of the above or a combination of monetary remuneration and time off in lieu of hours worked.

Medical insurance: This usually has two components: basic coverage and supplemental coverage. Some companies deduct the premium for basic coverage directly from an employee's base salary and offer the supplemental benefit (group insurance) either as an option for the employee to pay for or as a bonus. Other companies pay for the basic coverage and don't offer supplemental group coverage. The kinds of services included in the basic coverage will depend on the medical system in the country. Supplemental benefits may include coverage for dental and vision for the policy owner, spouse and dependents, as well as coverage for massage therapy, physiotherapy and chiropractors. Ask about the benefits and when they become effective. For example, company policy may stipulate that health benefits become effective after three months of continuous employment or slowly phased in during the first year.

Other benefits: These may include company contributions to retirement saving plans (in addition to mandatory contributions), stock options, paid sick days and bereavement leave (ask how many days), company-paid lunches, parking, birthday celebrations, Christmas parties or other events organized and sponsored by the company. Many companies will reimburse the expenses you incur while using your personal vehicle for business.

Negotiating a Compensation Package

Once you have received an offer, don't feel obliged to provide an answer on the spot. Take time to think about it. Legal wording in employment contracts may sound good when given a quick read but be deceiving once properly digested. There may be aspects you may not have noticed at first glance and you will be glad you took your time. Review all the details and give it at least one day before deciding what to do. Make sure you have a clear picture of what you can expect from your potential employer and what your employer expects of you.

During the negotiation, be articulate and answer questions directly and truthfully. Know your limits and abilities. (Note: you will be in an even better position to negotiate if you have at least two offers. If you don't have two good offers, I suggest you research the salary range for the position.)

VI. 3   Social Insurance Number

Look into getting a "social insurance number" or the equivalent. This is a unique number that every resident must have to obtain employment. Every employer will ask for this number before completing the hiring process. In some countries this is the only way to identify you for tax purposes. No matter how you earn income, you will need to register with the revenue agency or an equivalent ministry.

Learn as much as you can about how the social system works in your adopted country. Basically, having social insurance makes you eligible for two very important things: unemployment insurance and retirement income insurance. These represent your safety net for the present and future. If possible, obtain coverage for both. This will ensure you receive some income to cover your immediate expenses while continuing the search for a job (unemployment insurance) and later, when you reach retirement age (retirement income insurance). You can find more information about social security on the Internet.

VI. 4   Taxation

The taxation system varies from country to country, but it is crucial that you understand how it works. Of special interest are *tax brackets*, *tax levels* and *revenue declaration procedures for taxation*. Most employers will inform you of the "gross" value of your salary. What you receive after taxes are deduced is your "net income." The remuneration system, based on rules and regulation imposed by the labor ministry in cooperation with the revenue agency, retains the tax value from your salary before issuing you a paycheck or depositing your salary into your bank account. (In an earlier section I discussed what you should look for when opening a bank account. By now you should know what type of bank account you need and which bank will maintain your account.) In rare situations, you are paid the "gross" amount and it is your responsibility to make the tax payment as required.

The taxation system in certain countries can be confusing, so some people enlist the aid of an accountant or use custom computer software. Because taxation systems can be complicated, the support of a good financial advisor will also bring you peace of mind and free up precious time for you to settle into your new home. (More about the financial aspects in Chapters XI and XIII.)

Grants and Tax Refunds

Depending on which country you settle in, you may be eligible to receive certain government tax refunds or grants. For example, if you are a parent, you may be entitled to receive a grant up to a certain amount per month, per child. The value of the grant may depend upon your income. If you contribute to a "registered retirement savings plan," you may receive a tax exemption. In some countries, mortgage interest payments are deductible. Sometimes these refunds, grants or deductions are issued automatically by the financial system of the country. In other cases, you may need to apply and produce the required documentation before a refund or grant is issued. Contact the appropriate authority or ministry to request details on your eligibility, how you can apply and how the grant or refund will be issued. Your financial advisor, accountant or local Immigration office will direct you to the proper ministry or authority.

CHAPTER VII.

SCHOOLING FOR YOUR CHILDREN

I SUGGEST YOU plan well in advance and register your kids in the school of your choice as early as possible, even before you actually move. The school may ask for proof of residency (a rental or lease agreement, for example). Some schools have waiting lists in case there are more registration requests than available spaces, so consider registering your child(ren) in a second school as well.

You may prefer catholic or private schools to public ones. Each of them has a different focus and they fit better in one way or another depending on your plans for the future, lifestyle and beliefs. In addition, the costs differ from case to case. As you are probably aware, private schools are not free. Carefully analyze each option and choose the one that makes both common and business sense. For example, if you target a private school due to its prestigious curriculum but you cannot afford it now, start with a public school and save money for a future move to the private school. Some schools operate within predefined borders. This means that children living within the borders have priority over ones living outside the borders. In some cases, children living outside the borders are not even allowed to register.

Gather as much information as possible about the school(s). For example, what is the educational focus, objectives, methods, schedules and lunch program? Talk to people you know about the schools in your area. Ask them which school is better in their opinion, and why. Visit the schools, during and after classes. Observe how the teachers deal with the crowd when the first bell rings in the morning and after recess. See if the classrooms are clean and tidy. Arrange to speak to the teacher(s) who will be teaching your child(ren). Discuss any questions or concerns you may have.

Although in many countries public schooling is paid for by the government, there are some costs that parents incur during each school year. In many cases, school supplies must be paid for by parents. Alternatively, parents might choose to participate in a program organized by the school, which purchases supplies at discounted prices. The school curriculum might also include educational field trips to various places like museums, science centers, theatres, and so on. These trips can only take place if the parents reimburse the school with the total cost of these trips. Some schools run a supervised lunch program where children receive snacks and drinks.

Daycare and After-School Care

In some countries, it is illegal for children to be unsupervised by adults under a certain age (usually around eleven). Depending on the ages of your children and your work schedule, you may need to arrange for daycare or after-school care. The difference between the two is that a child spends the entire day in a daycare, as opposed to only several hours in the afternoon in the after-school care program. The after-school care facility is generally associated with the school. If it is not located in the same building as the school, adult caregivers accompany your children to the facility, where they engage in fun and entertaining activities with others of similar age under supervision. Keep in mind that waiting lists and border inclusion conditions may also apply to daycare and after-school care. After-school care is not free and the cost depends on the age of the child—higher for younger children and decreasing as the children get older. The same applies to daycare. Find out what the program includes. Since your children will most likely be hungry, ask if a snack is included with the fee. If their snack does not conform to your nutritional guidelines, ask them to exclude your child(ren) and then pack extra food in their school bags.

Another slightly more expensive way to ensure your child(ren) are in a safe environment during the day or after school is to hire a babysitter to look after them. He or she would pick them up at school, accompany them to your house and stay with them until you got home. To ensure the safety and protection of your children, I highly recommend that you verify the prospective babysitter's references and have the police department do a criminal check on him or her.

CHAPTER VIII.

MONTHLY EXPENSES

Tracking your Expenses

OF COURSE, YOU'LL want to monitor your monthly expenses in your new home. You can optimize the expenses by closely auditing all transactions at regular time intervals. One easy way of tracking your expenses is by using a bank card for all your purchases. This could be a *debit card* that is linked to your checking, savings or other account, or a *credit card* (Visa, MasterCard, American Express, Diner's Club, etc) issued by your bank. Most banks and credit card companies in modern countries around the world have on-line systems where you can check your account balances and transactions on the Internet. Some major banks even categorize your expenses on their monthly online or paper statements. If you are computer savvy, you may want to transfer the transactions from the bank online reporting system onto a spreadsheet. Alternatively, you could develop your own way of tracking the expenses (e.g., collect receipts and manually record individual expenses).

Consider dividing your expenses into categories. For example: entertainment, restaurants, health care, trips, sports, car insurance, bank fees, interest paid on credit, clothing, car payment, car repairs, gas, rent/mortgage, childcare, household articles, gifts and social events, education, technology (computer purchase, upgrade and repairs), Internet, phone, TV, etc. The categories that attract the majority of expenses will become evident once you roll up the expense for each category into monthly totals.

For your convenience I've created two spreadsheets, one to track individual expenses (the transactions table) and the other to capture the rolled-up totals by category (the rolled up values table). They can be downloaded from the Internet at www.theimmbook.org .

Please note that *these tables are provided as examples to help visualize the way expenses could be tracked.* **They should not be considered or used as accounting or investment tools.**

Controlling Expenses

The best way to keep your finances under control is to set a goal and then develop a plan to reach that goal. If, for example, you decide to save 500€ every month, revise your budget so that you spend 500€ less than you earn each month. If, for the past six months, you've been saving only 200€ every month, you'll need to identify the areas where you can save an additional 300€. If it becomes evident that you're spending too much on, say, designer clothing, consider purchasing your brand-name items from "outlets" or discount stores, where you'll pay between 30%-80% less, or taking advantage of savings during promotions and various special events throughout the year. Instead of purchasing major items for your house—couches, dining room set, desks, chairs, TV sets and even carpets—at retail outlets, search online or look in the Classified section of your local newspaper. There's a good chance you'll see many of these items for sale in good condition at a fraction of the regular retail price. In North America, you'll also find pre-owned (and occasionally collector) items of decent quality at a very reasonable price at many weekend "garage sales" and "flea markets," where bartering is encouraged.

Maintaining a home or car can become quite expensive unless you find ways to minimize the repair costs. If you need a plumber or an electrician, consider doing the repairs on your own or hiring a local handyman. A handyman or friend may also be able to help you install or fix your computer, TV, VCR, DVD player, audio system, furniture, flooring, or even your car (see Chapter X.)

CHAPTER IX.

INTEGRATION

AFTER YOU SETTLE in your new home, your main objective will be to "integrate" or blend into the new society. The activities involved in this process range from getting registered with the local authorities to finding employment, learning the culture, improving your speaking and writing skills in the local language, and finding leisure activities for you and your family.

IX. 1   Maintaining Permanent Residence Status

To confirm your resident status, you will need to go through all the steps identified in your immigration package, which will likely include getting social insurance and health insurance. In addition to meeting these mandatory requirements, I recommend you also get a driver's license and identification card (if available from the governing body) and open a bank account. Having a driver's license will make it easy for you to look for a job, visit new friends and do the things you love to do. After you have found a job, opened a bank account, and received your health card and perhaps an identification card to prove your residence status, you will then need to know what you can and can't do in order to maintain this status. For example, you may not be allowed to spend more than six months outside the country. Of course, there may be certain conditions under which you may be allowed to work overseas for an extended period of time without losing your resident status. I suggest you contact the appropriate agency—most likely the ministry or state department that deals with immigration—to get all the information you need on this subject.

As a permanent resident, you will have rights and responsibilities that will likely be the same as those of regular citizens—with the exception of perhaps voting procedures. For example, you may be allowed to vote in municipal or county elections but not in national elections. Knowing your rights will give you a clear understanding of the conditions under which you must operate. Be sure to read all the publications available on this topic.

IX. 2   Fitting in

Aside from logistical problems, moving to another country poses many cultural challenges. In addition to the language barrier, there is the potential for numerous cultural misunderstandings and conflicts.

Language and Culture

You may have worked hard to get good command of the new language before your arrival. However, because you were not immersed in the environment of your destination country, you do not "think" in your new language. In other words, whenever you want to say something, it automatically comes to mind in your mother tongue and then you translate it using your limited

vocabulary in the new language. Often word-for-word translations don't express what you really want to say. At times they
make no sense at all and can even be offensive! Your goal is
to shift from formulating ideas in your mother tongue to thinking in your new language. That way, you will be able to express yourself quickly and easily in casual conversation.

Once you have a job, you will communicate with your coworkers in meetings, by email, during presentations, etc. At
first, you will translate your ideas into the new language before expressing them verbally. This increases the amount of
processing your brain needs to perform. Most likely it will take
you some time to prepare written communication. Aside from
doing your job, you will spend a lot of time learning new pro-
cesses and procedures, adjusting to your new environment,
and demonstrating your capacity and competence in a foreign
language setting, all of which will be intellectually challenging, even for a highly qualified worker. (Don't be surprised if
you feel exhausted at the end of the day!) Your time management skills will be crucial, analytical skills highly valued and
task management and prioritization skills a must-have. If you
become overwhelmed or frustrated, don't be hard on yourself.
Try to find a solution for whatever is challenging you.

There is a difference between business and casual language. Although you may do well at work using limited vocabulary specific to your job, it is important to also develop casual
vocabulary. This is what you will use most of the time to network with friends and coworkers. Developing and maintaining good relationships is a key component of your success.
Although it is possible to find your way without a good network
of friends and coworkers, it is so much easier when you have
these connections and can rely on them when needed. This
is especially true when seeking employment.

The best way to receive proper language education is to
take special courses for newcomers. Unless you have already
had an opportunity to fully immerse yourself in the foreign en-

vironment, adapting your translation will need improvement. Some countries include language training as part of their assistance program for new immigrants. This may even be sponsored by the government free of charge. If such a service doesn't exist, you will need to register for a private language-training program. Another option is to take conversation and business communication classes, which focus on improving communication skills.

Look for opportunities to practice your speaking and writing skills. This is the best way to become proficient in express-ing yourself effectively and coherently. Communication is at the forefront of human interaction and its power should not be underestimated. Listen to the radio at home or in the car. Tune into a station that has a good balance between music and talking. Watch television—talk shows and interviews are particularly helpful. Try to understand the lyrics in the music; if your TV has "close-captioning" capability, turn it on and read what is being said while listening to how it is being said. Reading also helps to improve vocabulary and perfect sen-tence construction.

A word of caution is warranted here. If you really care about improving your language skills quickly, I advise you to restrict the amount of time you spend in places where you speak only your mother tongue—parties, barbecues, get-togethers with your buddies and old pals from your home country. I don't mean to imply that this is unhealthy; you need to spend time relaxing, having fun and recharging batteries. Just make sure you spend an equal amount of time interacting with people who speak the local language.

Learning about a new culture can be challenging at times. It requires spending time with people, and listening and learn-ing from them. Studying their history will also help—their prominent figures, leaders and heroes. Extend your research into the arts as well. Music, cinema and theater may have played a major role in shaping the present culture. Learn the local idioms (sayings), as they will help get your point across without the need for extensive explanations.

Language is always charged with cultural content. Learn how to say the right things in the right way. When learning the vocabulary, pay close attention to the sentence construction, pronunciation, tone and intonation. Changing the tone or intonation when expressing an idea, making a request or asking a question, could completely change the meaning of a sentence. Consider the implications of making statements or posing questions that are considered taboo or offensive. At first, keep things simple and quash your desire to impress. If you are unsure of the real meaning of a certain combination of words, it is better not to use them. Don't risk making a fool of yourself!

You will probably find that people will be polite, not only in a work setting but also during casual interaction. They will realize that their language is a second language for you and that you are not yet proficient in it. They will make every effort to understand what you are trying to say and will ask for clarification only when it becomes too confusing for them. The downside of this behavior is that you will never know for sure if you used your words correctly. At times you may inadvertently alter the meaning of a sentence or be misunderstood. Unless someone points out the errors, it will be very difficult for you to improve. As much as possible, ask your friends and coworkers to correct your mistakes. Although this might be difficult for you, it is a very efficient way to improve and have fun at the same time. (Of course, this works best if the language you are learning is your friend or coworker's first language.)

Some languages are very different from others and this extends not only to vocabulary but also to pronunciation. Pronunciation is important when learning any language. Sometimes it takes a considerable effort to get the sounds right. Don't be embarrassed if your peers chuckle at the way you pronounce some of your words. Just smile and ask them to show you how to express yourself correctly. That way you will demonstrate that you're not only open to communicating but also willing to improve. This will no doubt be appreciated by the locals who realize you're trying your best.

Being a funny guy in your native tongue doesn't necessary translate into your being funny in another language. But don't shy away from telling your stories anyway. The way you tell the story will bring some color to the conversation, and it's the easiest way to find out if your funny side works its magic in another language. Listening to and participating in many conversations will give you the confidence you need to start translating and adapting your old stories in the new language. Depending on the crowd, bringing new stories to the table may animate the discussion, spark some new ideas or open new avenues of conversation. Don't worry if you fail to connect with people in the way you had hoped. Keep in mind that the residents of your new country are no different from those in your homeland—they, too, have distinct personalities and personal preferences.

Nationalism and Multiculturalism

Most people feel patriotic and proud of the country in which they were born. The people living in your adopted country will also have the same dedication to their country. This has some social implications for new immigrants. Many countries that accept immigrants have rules, policies and even laws to help new immigrants integrate. Some governments demonstrate their support for immigration by promoting multiculturalism. This usually has a positive impact on how immigrants are seen and accepted in the new society. Be aware that conflicts can arise if there is no national policy that embraces foreign culture, education and religion or allows immigrants to practice their own culture and traditions.

Regardless of governmental support and programs, you may still not be welcomed with open arms by members of your new society. Remember, some people will be afraid of strangers, may consider you to be a threat to their lifestyle and security, or simply don't accept foreigners. Others will have nothing against your culture and way of life. The locals are accustomed to their environment and way of life. Interacting with immigrants can sometimes make them feel uncomfortable and their instinctual reaction is avoidance. Be aware of this when someone ignores you or suddenly cuts the conversation short. As mentioned before, the easiest way to identify foreigners is by listening to them. Because of this, I cannot overemphasize the importance of developing your language proficiency. This will make for a much easier, more seamless integration. Adopting the culture of your new society will also make your integration easier.

Social Interaction

Spending time with people has many advantages—not only does it allow you to unwind, relax and "recharge your battery," it improves your speaking skills. (As mentioned before, your new friends should be people whose first language is the language you are learning.) I'm sure you'll agree that having something in common with the people you interact with will make your social time even more enjoyable. I suggest you get involved in as many activities as you can. By becoming active in the community—playing sports, volunteering, etc.—you will also make new friends. Generally speaking, people do not like talking to strangers, so whenever possible ask someone you know to introduce you to new people in the community. Attending school is another way to meet like-minded people. At school, topics and issues are discussed, problems are solved and people get involved in group activities, homework, sports, etc. Being exposed to a variety of people and situations will *expand your network of friends* and further develop your language skills. As you become more proficient in your adopted language, you will no longer have to translate from your mother tongue and will begin to "think" in the new language. When you reach this stage, communicating becomes much simpler and you can concentrate on expanding your vocabulary.

There will be challenges while interacting with people at the bank, government offices, stores, your landlord, etc. You will need to learn how to interact with these people, how to make requests, formulate questions, etc. The services you are getting may be different than what you were used with, so you will need to ask for different things. Even in a somewhat relaxed setting (shopping, for example), you will likely experience some stress from your inability to formulate requests in a way the person behind the counter can understand. You could be at the pharmacy asking for medication to calm down your headache, trying to send a letter with confirmation of receipt and tracking, asking for spices in the market, buying flowers for your spouse, getting your pants hemmed at the tailor, or getting your car serviced. When a clerk asks, "How may I help you?" it is most frustrating having to struggle to explain through gestures what could easily be explained in a couple of words. I strongly suggest that you avoid this frustration and prepare the questions before you get there. Otherwise, you may end up conducting most of your business online, avoid stores, and spend too much time in front of the computer. This type of activity is not considered "social interaction."

What you need is exactly the opposite. You need to go out and interact with people. Do not be afraid to ask questions like "How do you ask for...?" You may be surprised by the positive response you'll get. No doubt they'd rather tell you than listen to a request they cannot understand. Besides, this is how you build relationships. You never know when you'll be back in that store. (Although you may think you'll never need to ask for the same thing again, I can almost guarantee that you will!) You'll then see a familiar face that may even smile at you! This is the kind of effort you'll need to make to integrate into your new society. Try this when you go shopping. Explain in your own way what you are trying to achieve or want to purchase and ask the person behind the counter how he or she would ask for it. Not only you will spark a discussion and practice speaking, you will also learn something new. Imagine how happy you'll be when you ask that same store clerk for a product the best way possible. There'll be no confusion and you'll get what you need quickly and easily.

Another aspect of your daily interaction with people that may raise your stress level and overload you is the way you relay to your friends what has happened to you in the past, yesterday, or earlier the same day—stories of disappointment, amazement or surprise, or just comments or observations. In the beginning you will find telling these stories a real burden. You'll struggle trying to explain how someone cut you off in traffic or what a gorgeous flower garden you saw, what you experienced while on vacation, etc. They are so easy to explain in your first language, but your new audience doesn't understand that language. My advice is to keep things simple at first, and ask for assistance. Ask your friends to help you translate what you would like to express. Don't shy away from asking them for help. By now, they should know that you're learning and that you're trying your best. Relax, enjoy the moment, and have fun!

CHAPTER X.

TRANSPORTATION

X. 1   Personal Vehicle: Luxury or Necessity?

GETTING FROM ONE place to another has become a necessity these days, not a luxury. This is especially true in North America, where suburban areas have quickly built up. This is even more evident in places where the population density is low and where homes are more spread out. Workers can leave the hustle and bustle of the city at the end of the day and enjoy country-like living in modern homes surrounded by lots of green space. People commute tens of kilometers to work every day, sometimes passing through large, busy metropolitan areas. This situation calls for a reliable means of transportation to take the eager worker back and forth at exact times. Most people purchase cars they can drive themselves rather than rely on public transportation or a friend or neighbor. The pressure is on now to choose fuel-efficient vehicles whenever possible.

Where you live in relation to your workplace, shopping mall, bank, school, childcare, and your family size are some of the considerations in determining whether or not you need a vehicle. For example, a single person living within a ten-kilometer radius of his or her workplace may not need a vehicle, while a family of four living in the suburbs with both parents working at opposite corners of the city and both kids in school would certainly benefit from one. Even if the single person lived further from work, he or she would not need a car if public transportation was easily accessible.

Car vs. Public Transportation

A factor you should keep in mind when deciding to buy a vehicle is the financial ramifications of owning and maintaining the vehicle. Looking at the numbers may not be the ultimate deciding factor, but it will help to build a complete picture of what you are up against. After you factor in all the conditions, constraints, and nice-to-haves, you'll be able to make an informed decision. Then, should any of the conditions under which you operate change, you can rethink the situation and make another decision.

Let's say, for example, a man (we'll call him John) does not own a car and uses public transportation to go to work. Based on John's current living expenses (which include a $100 monthly public transportation pass), a surplus of $600 is achievable every month. His goal is to deposit as much money as possible every month in a savings account, with a target of $600. Let's say John wishes to increase the comfort of his commute to work by purchasing a car. His vehicle of choice costs about $10,000 (comparative calculations have been made for $5,000 as well.)

The goal of the example is to identify the cost of comfort paid by John and how long it will take to amortize. If he cannot afford to purchase the car with one payment, he will need to purchase it on credit. In that case he will add to the car cost the interest and credit insurance costs. Even if the car is under warranty (which is not the case in this example), the following expenses will be incurred at regular intervals: gas ($60 - $100), auto insurance ($60 - $140), oil ($20 - $50), air filters ($10 - $30), tires ($100 - $300), brakes ($100 - $300), belts ($100 - $200), exterior washing ($5 - $15), interior cleaning ($20 - $140) and parking ($80 - $200 per month; this includes parking at your residence, at work and occasional temporary parking around the city). The warranty will only cover the occasional repairs ($100 - $200). These expenses can vary from country to country and even between suppliers and service providers in the same area.

The table below shows the cost distribution. An average value has been used (except for parking). Look for the corresponding prices in your area and update the numbers in the table to give you a true picture.

	Car purchase	Cost components			Public transportation
		Loan amount -->	$10,000	$5,000	
589 / month	**Monthly loan payment**	Principal *	325	162	**414 / month**
		Interest *			
		Insurance *	4	2	
	Insurance *		100	90	
50 / month	**Operation costs**	Gas *	80		**Monthly pass [100]**
		Parking *	80		
		Oil	35		
		Air filters	20		
		Brakes	200		**50 / month**
		Tires	200		
		Belts	150		
		Repairs	150		
		Exterior washing	10		
		Interior cleaning	80		

Note: * monthly expenses

Table 1 – Car ownership vs. public transportation

The value of the investment is considerable and will undoubtedly have a serious impact on John's ability to save a decent amount of money every month. His minimum monthly cost of owning a car is about $590. This takes into account gas, insurance, parking and a loan payment of about $325/

month for 33 months (including 5% interest). As you can see, the $600 that he was able to save in the beginning is now being used to pay for his car. In other words, he has traded his saved money for the freedom and comfort of owning a car.

Let's see if we can find a point in time where the car purchase would even out in relation to his bus pass expense. If John traveled by bus over a period of 100 months (eight years and four months at a rate of $100 per month), he would need to spend $10,000 (the car price). If we include the interest expense on his loan, it would take another six or eight months to equal the total borrowing cost, (depending on the interest rate). In other words, the money he paid for the car would eventually be spent on bus passes. After the loan is paid in full, the cost for gas, insurance, parking and maintenance (about $50 per month for an entry-level, low budget compact car) would still continue. Altogether, these expenses would total on average about $300 per month (over a two-year period). For single man John, these expenses could be considered a "comfort fee." In the case of the family of four, however, they are a necessity rather than a comfort.

It is clear that the monthly cost of owning a car is higher than the cost of a monthly bus pass and there will never be a brake-even point. Traveling by car will never be less expensive than traveling by bus. In fact, the lowest monthly cost that you can possibly incur with a low-maintenance car (which I recommend) is about $170. Of course, this amount could also be reached without owning a car if you choose to occasionally take alternative modes of transportation such as taxis, limos, etc.

The flexibility of owning a car is definitely a plus and a personal preference that may or may not take higher priority over saving $364 over the first 33 months (monthly ownership cost of $464 for the $5,000 loan, minus the bus pass cost of $100) and another $200 over the remaining 75 months (average, long-term monthly ownership cost as of month 34, minus the bus pass cost of $100), for a total of nine years of savings (the amortization period of 108 months to cover the total borrowing costs). The savings accumulated if you do not purchase a car would total about $27,000 (5,000 loan) and close to $33,000 (10,000 loan)—money you could invest wisely for your future.

Owning a car has social implications as well. You can help friends who do not own a car, take your date to a movie or restaurant and stop afterwards to listen to the rain while gazing at the city lights from a remote, elevated spot. With a car you can quickly and easily get to and from work, do your shopping and banking, take trips outside the city or visit friends. A car gives you the freedom to go from place to place at your own pace without having to follow bus or subway schedules.

Many people cannot imagine life without a personal mode of transportation. Be prepared to approach the situation with an open mind and analyze your options carefully.

X. 2   Purchasing a Car

Take your time selecting and purchasing a car. Review the options available on the market and identify the ones that match your expectations. Research car ratings online, including users' opinions and price. Read both users' and professionals' comments. Study the reviews so you're familiar with the products and their strengths and weaknesses. To search for these reviews on the Internet, type in "cars reviews." You'll be directed to a variety of sites that specialize in car reviews, reliability ratings and customer satisfaction surveys.

If you do not know where to start, I suggest looking at your priorities. Keep in mind that an efficient, reliable car will not only reduce your gas and maintenance costs but also your loan payments and insurance premiums (smaller cars). Do not overlook the fuel type (regular, premium, diesel, etc.)

Determine if you want a vehicle that is good-looking, reliable, or affordable. (Note: it is rare to find all three in one car!) Knowing which one of these characteristics takes priority will make things simpler for you. Give each of these priorities, as well as any others you identify, a rating from 1 to 5. This is called "grading." To give you a clear picture on how this works, take a look at the table below:

	Price	Looks	Reliability	
Priority -->	2	3	1	Score
Option 1	= 3 x 2	= 2 x 3	= 4 x 1	16
Option 2	= 5 x 2	= 4 x 3	= 2 x 1	24
Option 3	= 2 x 2	= 5 x 3	= 3 x 1	22

Table 2 – Car purchase decision matrix

The table points out that the "price" has a rating of 3 for Option 1, which could also be interpreted as a little over the average. Let's say you are prepared to spend a maximum of $10,000 (your budget) and you consider a very good deal to be $8,000 (a rating of 5). In our case, the car in Option 1 costs about $9,200 (a rating of 3). If we analyze the "looks," this car does not meet expectations so it received a 2 rating. You have ascertained that this car is reliable, so it received a rating of 4. After filling out the table with the ratings of the other options, I multiplied the individual ratings by the priority then added the totals in each cell to obtain a final score per option. In this case, Option 2 had the highest score. This car is not reliable, but it meets the other priorities, with a rating of 5 for price and 4 for looks. In other words, this car is an inexpensive, good-looking lemon. On the other hand, a priority of 3 for reliability implies less maintenance (lower maintenance costs), resulting in lower total cost of ownership. Even if this car costs more to purchase, you will recover the money by avoiding repairs and time wasted in service centers. Reliable cars also have a better resale value (when you sell the car, you recover more of the money you paid at purchase).

Purchasing a car can become a daunting experience if you have never been involved in negotiations or are not one of those people who are constantly buying and selling things. Having some negotiation experience will help because buying a car always involves negotiation to some degree. A car is considered a large-ticket item that is usually purchased on credit. A decent used car will cost around $10,000. While you may think this is a lot of money, I advise that you don't buy a cheaper one given the problems you may incur because of the car's age or condition.

There may be good deals available at first sight, but before you jump in, consider the cost/quality ratio. The "look" should be a "nice-to-have," not a prerequisite. There are pros and cons for any car and only you should decide which one works best for you. Don't let someone else make the decision for you. You want to get the most out of your dollar. This will be one of your first long-term investments in your dreamland. Don't base your decision solely on a dealer's recommendations. The car dealer has a vested interest in selling the cars in stock. If the dealer does not have the car you want in stock, go somewhere else. If possible, make an environmentally friendly choice. Apart from their impact on the environment, you'll spend less money on gas (which means more money in your pocket) and on consumables (tires, filters, oil, brake pads, etc.) Smaller cars are also easier to park and maneuver though traffic and narrow streets.

Looking for a low-cost parking spot while you are at work will also help to reduce your expenses. Even if located further away from your workplace, it may be worthwhile in the long run (savings accrued over time), plus you will have the opportunity to enjoy a morning and afternoon walk! While you research your options, take note of the parking lot location and surroundings and ensure the savings are not offset by expenses due to vandalism or theft.

Dealer vs. Private Purchase

Cars may be purchased either from a dealer or from a private person. No matter how you purchase your car, you will save thousands of dollars if you plan your purchase properly and stick to the plan throughout the negotiation. If you don't feel confident enough or just aren't ready to negotiate, get help from a friend. Discuss the details, including the car specifications and target price. Make sure your friend follows the plan closely. Since your friend is not paying out any money, he or she will not be emotionally attached to the car. Skilled salespeople can sense your attachment to a certain product and can lead the discussion towards maximizing their profits. This is why you should conduct the purchase in a relaxed manner without showing any attachment to any product. Do all your research beforehand, and don't go to the dealership unless you've made your decision. Know exactly what you are looking for! Be somewhat flexible, but set your limits and stick to them. You will rarely find exactly what you are looking for because your product may not match exactly what the dealer has in stock. The dealer may also want to sell what he has more of or what is being priced at a higher margin.

If you wish, you can purchase a car from a private person. On the Internet are numerous websites dedicated to buying and selling cars by region and even by city. There are also local publications available online and in print where you'll find a large selection of vehicles for sale. The only disadvantage I see when you purchase a car from a private owner is that he or she will sell the car "as is." Dealers are generally required by law to guarantee that a car is in good working condition and has passed certain safety tests, or clearly specify the car is sold "as is." This, of course, varies from country to country. Unlike buying from dealers, buying from a private person makes *you* responsible for ensuring the car is in good working order. You'll need to run all the necessary tests to ensure the car is safe to drive. You'll need to arrange this with the seller as a condition for purchase or look into it yourself after the purchase. If a car is sold as is, once the sale is closed (the ownership is transferred and the money paid), you cannot go back and claim any kind of compensation for defects, damage or injury incurred after the sale. This is why it is so important to ensure the car is safe for the road and in good working condition before taking your family for a ride.

I don't recommend you go shopping for a car from a private owner without knowing how to do some basic checks to ensure the car is free of serious problems. If you do not have experience with cars, seek help from a friend or someone you trust. A rule of thumb: if a deal seems too good to be true, it probably is. "Good deals" usually come with a catch that you find out about only after the sale is complete. If you cannot get someone to help and you do not know cars, I suggest you buy from a dealer and ask about the warranty terms and conditions. The warranty will bring you peace of mind.

If you feel strongly about saving some extra bucks and purchasing from a private owner, I suggest you search the Internet for tips and tricks about buying cars. Type in "car purchase tips." You may also want to ask the seller to take the car to a mechanic of your choice for a quick check. Always be prepared. Consider the money you will be paying and how much you have worked to earn it. Consider your safety and the safety of others on the road.

Car Insurance and Registration

Upon completing the purchase, you must register your car. Some dealers offer this as an added service. They will register the car in your name and get registration plates in addition to obtaining all the road safety certifications. If the dealer does not register the car for you, or if you have purchased the car from a private owner, you will have to take care of the registration yourself. The registration process varies from country to country. For information and requirements, contact the Ministry of Transportation or other body in charge of road safety and transportation regulations. Also inquire about the child car seat regulations. There are differences between car seats based on the age of the children riding in them. Infant car seats, for example, are built so the baby faces the back of the car, which has been determined the safest seating option for small babies.

In order to register your car, you must have already purchased car insurance. (In most places, this is the law.) *You should begin researching your insurance options even before you purchase the car.* Basic coverage generally includes "third party liability" insurance, which means that you do not have to pay for the damage you cause to other vehicles or property when you are at fault. This option does not cover repairs to your own vehicle. (For more information on basic and optional insurance coverage, search the Internet for "auto insurance basics.")

Once you have narrowed down the options, you can initiate dialogue with an insurer. Pay attention to what is included in the insurer's offer. Sometimes an insurance company will "bundle" options with the basic coverage, so the premiums may seem high. Find out what is included in the basic coverage and decide if you need any of the other options. For example, if you believe you need coverage for repairs to your car in case of an accident where you are at fault and the premium for this is not very high, I suggest you add it. This optional coverage is sometimes referred to as "collision coverage." Your insurance premium will be adjusted according to which option(s) you choose. The premiums will vary, depending on the car's brand, age, model, engine size, or a combination of these. The premiums will generally be higher for cars that are preferred by car thieves and ones that are more expensive to repair. Normally, the older the car, the lower the insurance premium, excluding vintage cars. (Keep in mind these rules may not apply everywhere.)

Don't jump to conclusions if the quotes are higher than you expected. The insurance companies are in business to make money and will try to sell you as many products as possible. It is your responsibility to know exactly what you are purchasing. Before choosing the lowest-priced offer, investigate how quickly the respective insurance company responds to a claim and how quickly they refund money to claimants. Ask what happens if you are involved in a traffic accident. For example, will they cover expenses incurred to transport the car from the location of the accident to a repair shop? Ask what repair shops they work with in your city and if they will pay for repairs. If they refund you the money for repairs, how long will you have to wait before the refund is issued? Also ask if they will cover your costs for alternative transportation while your car is being repaired.

Car-related expenses that you should pay attention to are: the loan payment, gas, insurance, parking and car maintenance. In most situations, the second biggest monthly car expense (after the loan payment) is the insurance premium. To minimize the cost, I suggest you shop around. The time you initially spend on finding low-cost insurance will pay off in the long run. Keep in mind that insurance companies rate drivers based on their driving records and experience (length of time they've had a driver's license). Higher ratings come with lower premiums, and vice-versa.

While you are researching your options for insurance, keep in mind that professions in certain industries or members of certain professional organizations may be eligible for discounts. If you have earned a professional designation or are a member of a professional group recognized at the national or international level, make sure to point out to the insurer your status and ask if you can take advantage of any discounts. In addition, your membership to certain clubs may entitle you to discounts on various purchases, including insurance.

Car Maintenance

Earlier on in this chapter, I estimated that it will cost approximately $50 every month to maintain a car, for a total of $600 per year. Of course, this depends on the reliability and age of the car. It also depends on the repair shop's rates and quality of workmanship.

Finding a repair shop that you can trust to make reliable, effective repairs is not an easy task (that is, the technician fixed it properly and the repairs don't require revisiting or adjustment.) Most car manufacturers or dealerships charge high rates, and even then, it may not be long before you need to go back to check the car for the same problem or a new one that just surfaced. Often it takes too long to fix the car.—parts must be ordered and they don't arrive in a timely fashion. Dealing with repair shops can quickly become a frustrating experience!

In all fairness, I should say that the work of an automotive service technician and mechanic has evolved from being simply mechanical to being highly technological, where integrated auto electronic systems and complex computers run vehicles and measure their performance on the road. Service technicians and mechanics must continually adapt to changing technology and repair techniques as vehicle components and systems become increasingly sophisticated.

So, how do you go about finding a trustworthy repair shop? First of all, look for one that is associated with a major parts supplier and that the supplier has competitive prices on the parts it is selling. This will somewhat guarantee that they won't keep your car in the shop too long while waiting for a part to arrive. Regarding the quality of workmanship and diagnostics accuracy, ask friends, neighbors and colleagues where they regularly take their cars for servicing. It may be that preventive maintenance is done at a different location than the repair work. As with a lot of other businesses, auto maintenance and repair is organized by category: body shops, shops that specialize in oil change, brakes, mufflers, glass repair, etc. Some establishments do offer full service under one roof.

It is important to note that some repair shops will perform a quick diagnostic and then provide a repair estimate. They will proceed with the repair only if you agree with the estimate. *This quote does not legally bind the repair shop to providing the repair at the value on the quote.* This is because they could potentially discover other unrelated issues while solving the problem you reported and may have to resolve these other problems first before they can resolve the main problem that brought you to their shop initially. Although this usually doesn't happen, they could take advantage of this and suggest other costly repairs that may not be necessary. This is why it is usually a good idea to get quotes from various repair shops. Once you know exactly what is causing the problem, you can ask for estimates to fix or replace that particular part. If you are technically inclined, you may want to point out some of the issues to the technician and ask him/her to focus the checkup activities on the area of concern. Once you have provided your insight into the problem, the technician should resolve the issue to your satisfaction. If the repair is stable and you do not experience other related problems afterwards, you have found a good repair shop.

Certified mechanics who operate privately can also resolve some of your vehicle problems. These people take pride in their ability to resolve car problems at a low cost with high quality workmanship. If you happen to know one, at least get his opinion on what might be causing the problem. He will tell you how much it will cost to fix it at a repair shop compared to what he will charge for the same job.

Again, it becomes a matter of trust. If he seems genuine and honest, consider giving him a chance to prove what he can do. If someone you know has utilized his services, ask your friend for feedback on his work.

X. 3   Public Transportation

In most cities, public transportation is easily accessible and relatively inexpensive. The most commonly used methods of exchanging money for transportation services are tickets and monthly passes, although in some cities, you can also deposit coins (usually the exact amount of the fare) when you board the bus. Most of the time if you buy a bus pass you save money over a given period of time and you are allowed to travel as many times as you want within that period. To purchase a monthly pass, for example, you would pay a flat fee that is based on two trips per day for thirty days. Tickets are regularly sold at special outlets or via a network of authorized dealers. Passes are normally sold only at special outlets and may require your photo.

I suggest you obtain a complete list of the transportation service providers in your area, their ticketing policies and routing information and then determine all the ways to get to work or the shopping centre, etc. If one twenty-minute trip costs you $2 and another trip leading to the same destination takes only ten minutes at a cost of $4, you may want to consider the more expensive route if you are under time constraints. Remember, your time is valuable, and the more you spend in public transportation the less time you have for more important matters. The Victoria Transport Policy Institute prepared a very interesting study on transportation costs and benefits. If you are interested in reading more about the real cost of transportation, read this study at http://www.vtpi.org/tca/tca0502.pdf

Finding what bus to take should not be a daunting task. Most transportation providers have developed easy-to-use online routing information systems. Their websites are designed to allow travelers to easily find the bus numbers and best routes to get around the city. They also list the connection points for intersecting routes. This is useful when you need to change buses, transfer from bus to train, and so on. Another way to find out the best route is by asking people for directions. The locals are usually quite helpful.

Bus Trips to Other Destinations

Not owning a car should not stop you from traveling outside the city. Most transportation systems extend well beyond the city limits and sometimes include trains and/or airplanes. It may even be more cost-effective to travel 500 kilometers by plane than by car or bus. So keep your eyes open and don't rule out this option when comparing various possibilities. When booking travel outside a city, you will likely need to contact special companies that offer long distance travel services. Find out if you need a reservation and if the seats are guaranteed and numbered. If they are not (which may be the case on buses), you'll need to get there in advance to occupy your preferred seat. Arriving too close to the departure time may leave you with few options as far as seating goes or without a seat at all.

Be sure to get the right information, ask the right questions, plan in advance, and be prepared!

X. 4   Biking: the Environmental Choice

Governments and businesses all around the world have begun encouraging people to use alternative means of transportation due to the impact cars have on the environment. But reducing the amount of pollution is not the only benefit of using an alternative means of transportation. Two other benefits are staying fit and saving money. Medical test results have indicated that physical activity decreases mortality rates and the risk of cardiovascular disease mortality, maintains normal muscle strength, joint structure and joint function, appears to relieve symptoms of depression and anxiety, and improves mood. Considering all this, it may not make sense to use any other means of transportation but the bike. Unfortunately, however, the pace of life these days doesn't always allow us to spend sixty minutes commuting to work on a bike when the same distance could be traveled in ten to fifteen minutes.

If you would like to learn more about the bike as an alternative to motorized transportation, visit http://www.kenkifer.com/bikepages/advocacy/autocost.htm.

CHAPTER XI.

LIFESTYLES

XI. 1   Urban vs. Suburban Living

WHY DO SOME people choose to live in the suburbs rather than in the city? There are advantages and disadvantages to both, some of which I will list to help you decide which is best for you and your family.

Living in the city

Upside:

- 0   walking distance to shopping malls, schools, cinemas, clubs and banks
- 0   likely won't be driving as much because of the proximity to public transportation
- 0   greater cultural diversity: museums, libraries, theatres; many things to see and do
- 0   many places are open 24/7 or close later than in the suburbs

0   can have better schools (depends on the area); designer shops and lots of variety

Downside:

0   pollution, crowded streets, traffic, street noise
0   noise from neighbors (if living in an apartment building)
0   more people
0   higher crime rate
0   lineups almost everywhere you go
0   difficult to find parking
0   no escape from the crowds if you get tired of being around people

Living in the suburbs

Upside:

0   more space (depending on the property)
0   may have your own garden (potentially available in the city, too)
0   quiet at night (potentially available in the city, too)
0   peaceful setting (depending on the property you choose)
0   cleaner air
0   lower property costs (depending on the property and area)
0   less people and traffic noise

Downside:

0   more driving costs (car maintenance, gas, etc.)
0   time lost in traffic getting to and from work
0   everyone knows everyone

0   can be too quiet at night if you are young and very
     active
0   lacking one-stop shops, diversity, fashion and
     trendiness

If you are still undecided and wish to further compare the
two options, I suggest you look at the social and economical
aspects over a longer period of time (three to five years, for
example).

For more information on the social implications of urban ver-
sus suburban living, visit http://www.ceosforcities.org/. Here you
will find a study entitled "Attracting College-Educated, Young
Adults to Cities" conducted in 2006 by The Segmentation
Company, a division of marketing consultancy Yankelovich Inc.
Enter the study name in the search field to bring it up.

XI. 2   Renting vs. Buying a Home[*]

To rent or buy? That is the question! Most people choose to
buy because of the space and comfort their own home brings.
When you own a house you are free to make whatever changes
inside the house as long as the house remains structurally
sound. You can also make changes outside the house as long
as the changes are in accordance with the city's guidelines and
urbanism plan, and you can receive local community's acceptance. Many people choose to buy because house values generally appreciate and there's a good chance they will recover
the money paid on the mortgage upon selling the house. Other
people buy homes to gain social status, privacy and for safety
or security reasons.

---

[*]   The values used for calculations in this section are purely meant to drive the formulas
and help the reader understand the variables in connection with purchasing or renting
a house. The numbers used and assumptions made are based on data collected by the
author through research and from various sources including but not limited to friends,
family, studies, reports, and personal experiences. The formulas used in this section can
be studied by retrieving the spreadsheet from the author's web page www.theimmbook.
org. The information in this section has not been endorsed by any financial institution or
advisor; please consult a financial advisor for factual information.

Some people feel they can't afford a mortgage payment plus all the other expenses involved with ownership. In order to help you visualize what home ownership involves versus home rental, I've created the chart below:

House Ownership	Cost components	Rental
Mortgage	Principal	Rent
	Interest	
	Insurance (1)	
Property taxes		
Maintenance costs	Repairs	
	Grass cutting	
Community fees	Garbage pickup	
	Snow removal	
Utilities	Water	Rent (2)
	Electricity	
	Natural gas	
Homeowner insurance		Insurance (3)

(left margin: 40-45% of the mortgage value)

Notes:
(1) zero if down payment is more than 20% of house value
(2) some landlords include the utilities costs in the rent charges
(3) some landlords will require proof of insurance from tenants prior to move-in

Table 3 – Home ownership vs. home rental costs

To get an estimate of the costs in this chart (excluding the mortgage payment) use a popular search engine to look up "home ownership costs" on the Internet. The costs vary from country to country and from city to city. Based on data I found to be true where I live, I used costs in the range of 40% to 45% of the mortgage value.

It is important to note that a good part of your mortgage payment represents interest on the mortgage. Banks usually structure mortgages so that the payments during the first few years consist mostly of interest charges, with only a minimal contribution to the principal amount of the loan during that time. These charges decrease as time goes by and more of each payment is applied to the principal amount. For example, for the first seven years in a twenty-year mortgage of $100,000 (based on an interest rate of 5.5%), the interest will take up more than 50% of the mortgage payment. Think of this interest as "rent paid to the bank." Every payment you make builds up "equity" in your home that can be applied to the purchase of a larger house or your retirement. In addition, house values generally appreciate over time above inflation levels. Selling your house may allow you to pay the remaining mortgage balance and be left with some profit on top of that.

If you move around a lot or must relocate often for your work, you might want to consider renting. If the rent for your apartment includes all utilities, you wouldn't have to stop and restart electricity, water and heating services when you move. Your belongings would likely fit into one truck that you can drive yourself. If you're lucky, as I was, you could ask your friends to move the heavier items. Renting gives you the flexibility to take on new employment challenges without delay. Once relocated, you could find a temporary place to rent while looking for a more permanent solution. If, on the other hand, you were moving out of a house you owned, you would incur fees (anywhere between 3% and 7% of the house value) if you hired a real estate agent to handle the sale on your behalf. (To get an idea of the effort involved in a move, review the checklist available at https://ssl.postescanada-canadapost.ca/smartmoves/checklist/default-e.aspx.) Keep in mind that if you rent, you will be asked to sign an agreement, undergo an approval process (credit and reference check) and provide payment for the first and last month's rent (or first month's rent plus a security deposit) in advance. As a tenant, you would not be responsible for maintenance or repairs to the premises but would be required to abide by the rules and regulations specified in the rental agreement, one of which is giving your landlord advance notice before leaving.

As you can see in the above chart, there are expenses associated with home ownership that renters don't have to pay or are included in their monthly payment. In order to paint a clear picture of the financial implications of owning a home, I calculated the total monthly expenses that would typically be incurred by homeowners for a mortgage of $200,000 amortized over a period of thirty years at 6.5%. I did not include the principal in the calculation given it represents money saved rather than spent. First, I added together the interest paid in the first twenty years and 45% of the mortgage value, which includes property taxes, maintenance costs, community fees, utilities and homeowner insurance. Then I divided the result by twenty (years) and then by twelve (months per year). The result was $1,500, which represents an average monthly cost of owning this home. (Note: this situation would change in the last ten years of the mortgage when the average monthly cost would be about $950.) Here is the breakdown:

	First twenty years (monthly expense)	Last ten years (monthly expense)
Interest (at 6.5%)	$895	$336
45% of mortgage ($1,374)	$618	$618

The detailed calculations are in a spreadsheet, which you can download at www.theimmbook.org

The Housing Market

The housing market is volatile. Many factors influence housing prices, including the health of the local economy, the job market, as well as economic, political and social factors. While the stock market tends to be very volatile (it goes up and down more frequently), the housing market has longer cycles and therefore is less volatile.

If you are planning to buy a house, you should know where you are in the cycle. Studies have shown that interest rates and house prices are on opposite sides of the spectrum. Some people believe that it's better to buy when interest rates are high and house prices are relatively low than when interest rates are low and house prices are relatively high. Investing in a house should not be taken lightly. A house is one of the biggest purchases you will ever make. If you purchase the house at the end of an upstream cycle you will find yourself paying a huge amount of money for a long time and may not be able to take advantage of its appreciating value. This is because when you are at the top of a housing bubble, the value will remain steady or even decrease and may never catch up with your interest payments. Even if it does catch up, your earnings may not be as high as they could be.

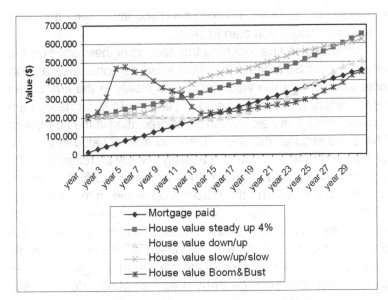

Table 4 – Housing market ups and downs

The above chart demonstrates how a house's value can increase over time. The purchase price for the house in this chart is $200,000 with a mortgage over 30 years, 6.5% annual interest, and no downpayment. The diagonal line beginning at 0 represents the mortgage paid (cumulative). The diagonal line starting at 200,000 represents a possible year-to-year house value appreciation, up 4%. (A color chart is available at www.theimmbook.org). The average annual house price appreciation in the United States of America has been around the 4.5% mark over a ten-year period (http://www.scribd.com/doc/3675696/US-National-Association-of-Realtor-Statistics-19682008-Annual-Home-Appreciation-based-on-the-median-price-of-homes-sold-62508 and http://www.free-books.us/us_national_association_of_realtor_statistics_1968_2008_median_price_on_home_sales_6_25_08.php&free_ebook=3675699). In some markets around the world this value is higher and could go to even 10% over shorter periods of time. In other markets this value is much lower and has not increased in years. I recommend you investigate the rates in the area where you plan to settle.

The turquoise line reaching the second highest point on the chart in year 30 labeled "slow/up/slow" demonstrates a probable trend where the value increases slowly in the first seven years before rapidly increasing in years eight to fourteen, then slowing down to a below-average appreciation in the final years. This trend secures the second highest market value at the end of the mortgage term with an average yearly increase of 3.9%. The yellow line slowly going downwards in the first 12 years labeled "down/up" and then picking up slowly in the remaining years with a peak in year 24 is the second slowest performer on the chart. This shows that a market with negative appreciation after the house has been purchased is indicative of minimal earnings over the total paid to the bank in mortgage payments. In this case the average annual appreciation rate is 3.16%. Lastly, the purple line with a steep increase in the year two to four and labeled "Boom&Bust" is representative of a booming economy with impressive earnings in the boom years and then gradual depreciation in the eight years that follow. The market returns to average earning levels in the second half of the mortgage term when the value appreciates steadily but does not overrun the total paid in mortgage payments. In this case the average annual appreciation is 2.75%. These examples do not take into consideration inflation or natural adjustments due to market-inflated prices. Since it is difficult to estimate when or if such adjustments might take place throughout the lifetime of a mortgage, I chose not to show it. If house prices rise too quickly, people cannot afford to buy. A lack of demand will drive prices down to more affordable levels.

Prior to purchasing a home, it's important for you to understand how inflation will affect its value over time and how interest rates will affect the mortgage amortization period and your regular contributions. (To learn about all the variables related to buying a home, review the homebuyer checklist at http://www.ourfamilyplace.com/homebuyer/first.html.) In the example above (steady up 4%), the purchase price was $200,000 (the Present Value). At the end of thirty years, if we take the average 4% annual appreciation, the house value will be about $650,000 (the Future Value), a 325% gain. However, this amount of money may not be enough to purchase three houses, as you might think. Once we factor in inflation (2.5% per year, for example), the actual appreciation is only 155%. This equates to $310,000. Furthermore, if we deduct the total amount of interest paid over the thirty years ($255,000), we are left with only $55,000 (the actual gain in today's money from selling this house thirty years from now).

In the example above, a person willing to purchase a $200,000 house (that appreciates 4% annually) must be earning a minimum annual income of about $71,000. Unless that person's salary also increases by at least 4% annually, it will not keep pace with the house appreciation and therefore decrease his or her purchasing power over time. As a result, this person will not afford to buy the same house several years later.

More details on the effects of the inflation, formulas to calculate the present value, and discussions on rent vs. mortgage are available on the Internet at www.theimmbook.org

XI. 3   Selling your Home

At some point in the future, you may want to sell your house. The decision to sell could be triggered by your finding another job in another area, a need to upgrade to a newer and/or larger house in the same area, or a desire to move into a similar home in a nicer neighborhood, closer to work, school, shopping malls, etc. By selling your house, you'll hopefully pay off your mortgage and make a profit. Before you sell, keep these things in mind:

a) Most people choose to use real estate agents, whose

fees range from 3% to 7% of the selling price. This will be deduced from the proceeds of the sale.

Real estate agents will help you set the selling price of your house, advertise, find buyers, complete buy/sell contracts, etc. More details can be found at http://www.bls.gov/k12/money05. htm or by searching the Internet for "Definitions of real estate agent." Public notaries or lawyers will prepare the legal documentation that confirms the transfer of ownership to the buyer. Ask friends and acquaintances to refer you to a lawyer they trust. Helpful hint: price is not always indicative of the quality of service.

b)   Most houses in your area will have also risen in value.

If you paid $100,000 for a house ten years ago and the mortgage term is twenty years, there would be another ten years left to pay if you decided to sell today. The remaining mortgage balance would be about $82,000, if the mortgage interest rate is 5.5%. If you choose to upgrade to a bigger house in the same area, the value of the house you want to buy will be higher than the sale price of your house today. (Nicer, bigger and/or better means pricier!) Consequently, you will have to make up the difference by either borrowing money (obtaining another mortgage) or using money you've saved. The only way you can take advantage of house appreciation is if you move to another area where house prices are lower.

In the process of switching houses, you will have an opportunity to change lenders. The amortization period (the actual number of years it will take to pay back your mortgage) or monthly mortgage payments are lower when the interest rate is lower. Shop around for a trustworthy, reliable, reputable lender with a solid track record who can offer competitive mortgage packages.

A more detailed discussion and calculations can be reviewed online at www.theimmbook.org

Part III - Advancing Through the Mist

CHAPTER XII.

LEARNING AND LIVING IN YOUR NEW COMMUNITY

ONCE YOU'VE ARRIVED in your new home, the number of issues to be addressed and information to be processed will likely be overwhelming. I found it helpful to formulate an action plan. If you apply this concept to your day-to-day life, you'll find that you will accomplish more in a day, week or month. Many people I've met attribute their success to careful planning and being organized.

My action plan includes the following steps:

0   set "possible" and "achievable" objectives
0   identify action items to accomplish objectives
0   assign a finite time interval for each action item
0   make note of potential challenges or roadblocks that may surface while identifying the action items
0   define specific action items that address challenges
0   identify activities that cannot yet be broken down into concrete action items (more details may surface along the way)

Once you review the newly built plan, the objectives previously classified as "possible" might become "achievable." You will also know if you are going in the right direction. Don't waste time and energy heading towards a dead-end. While collecting information to develop the action items, you'll become aware that other people's feedback is relative to each individual's situation. Consequently, you analyze the feedback received to ensure it will help you reach your objectives. As you move forward, you will encounter obstacles, but try not to get discouraged. Remain positive, despite the obstacles, and look forward to what lies ahead. Be flexible and open to new possibilities!

In the sections that follow, I cover some of the common issues that new immigrants will likely face in their new communities.

XII. 1 Health Concerns

Moving from one place to another can have a significant impact on your health. Your body is accustomed to living in a particular environment, eating certain foods, etc. and can react negatively to any change. For example, you may get headaches in response to a change in diet or barometric pressure. You could develop respiratory problems because of a change in air quality or from being subjected to new viruses. If you or other members of your family suffer from asthma or other respiratory problem, be sure to investigate the air quality before you move to your new destination. The same goes for any other conditions you have that will require monitoring. Maintaining good health will prevent or lessen the impact of these changes on your body. As most of you already know, the best way to stay healthy is to get regular exercise, practice good hygiene, eat a healthy diet and get plenty of sleep. Later in this chapter I will discuss how changes in the food industry have affected many of the products you'll find in grocery stores.

XII. 2 Environmental Issues

Electromagnetic Fields

Most people are not aware (or ignore the fact) that modern technology also has an impact on our health. In the modern world, we are surrounded by electronic devices. Have you ever wondered how they affect our body?

Every day we are immersed in a sea of electromagnetic waves generated by cell phones, cell phone base stations, signal amplifiers, cell phone towers, microwave ovens, house wiring, transformer-based power adapters, wireless routers, automobiles, etc. Having said this, not all the electromagnetic fields surrounding us are dangerous to our health. Over the years, studies have been conducted to identify the field intensity safety threshold. Published maximum exposure limits vary from country to country. The debate continues as to what electromagnetic field (EMF) level is considered safe. Many government and utility documents report a typical ambient level of 60-Hz magnetic field to be 0.5 mG (milligauss). I consider 0.1 mG to be safe enough and try to limit my exposure to higher levels. Governments and universities around the world have invested in research to identify the links between exposure to electromagnetic fields and human health. The research has identified some safe exposure limits and suggested that prolonged exposure to electromagnetic fields over the safe threshold can result in health problems. New studies have linked cell phone radiation to brain tumors, cancer, and cellular damage. (For more information on this subject, visit http://www.mercola.com/article/emf/emf_dangers.htm.) Generally speaking, prolonged exposure to any field over the threshold is not recommended. The Environmental Protection Agency in the U.S. (EPA) has proposed a safety standard of 1 mG. Sweden has set a maximum safety limit of 1 mG.

There are devices on the market that measure field strength. These devices come in various models, depending on the frequency of the waves in the field. The fields produced by electrical wires and transformers could be 50 or 60 Hz (low frequency), depending on the continent. On the other hand, fields produced by cell phone antennas have a higher frequency (850MHz). You can read more about the influence of electromagnetic fields on the human body at http://www.emfacts.com/papers/cfs.html and http://www.feb.se/ARTICLES/electrosmog.html. Information on thresholds is also available through various publications accessible on the Internet. Use the following key words or a combination of them: "emf," "emf exposure," or "emf limits." If you are interested in purchasing detectors, search using the key words "electrosmog emf meter."

I would be remiss if I didn't mention the risk of exposure to an EMF produced by high-voltage power lines. In order to limit the potential loss of power over long distance, operators raise the voltage to 110 KV (kilovolts) or more. These lines provide power to substations, where the power is stepped down to lower levels for regional distribution and then to the levels used in our houses (110V or 220V, for example). Unfortunately, the high voltage of the alternating current passing though these lines creates a powerful electromagnetic field (EMF) around them. As mentioned, electromagnetic fields can have a negative impact on people's health if they exceed acceptable limits. Research has shown that there is a statistical link between EMF from power lines and leukemia and adult brain cancer. Even more than 200 meters away, their presence can have an effect on your health. If you would like more information on this subject, search the Internet using the key words "power lines health."

Soil Contamination

Before you commit to purchasing your new home, I strongly suggest you have it thoroughly inspected by a professional. This includes taking samples of the soil underneath the house. The composition of the soil will tell you a lot about its stability over time and whether or not it could potentially emit harmful gases that could penetrate your house, alter the air quality around the house, or even worse, cause your house to sink as the decomposed material compresses under the pressure of the soil on top.

Sometimes there are harmful gases in the soil that humans cannot detect. In many populated areas the uranium content of the rock underground is high enough to have a negative influence on people's health. The danger is not through exposure to radioactivity but through inhalation of the radioactive gas radon. Uranium is the first element in a long series of decay that produces radium and radon. Uranium is referred to as the "parent element," and radium and radon are called "daughters." With further decay, more "daughters" are produced. The newly made daughter products of radon include polonium, bismuth, and lead. Polonium is also radioactive. This element, which is produced by radon in the air and in people's lungs, can hurt lung tissue and cause lung cancer. This information was published by The Energy Resource Surveys Program of the U.S. Geological Survey and was still available at the time of writing this book at http://energy.cr.usgs.gov/radon/georadon/2.html.

As with most other harmful elements, radon won't have an immediate effect on your family's health. Its effects are cumulative and develop over time. It is also worth noting that radon concentration increases in poorly ventilated areas like basements. The gas infiltrates through cracks and accumulates in greater concentrations over time. The concentration of radon in your house can be measured with a special device. This measurement is not instantaneous; after installation, the unit must be left for a few days. If you detect radon, take action immediately. This may involve properly ventilating the area so that radon will continually be eliminated.

Most areas in North America have maps indicating the concentration of uranium. I suggest you study the map for the area in which you plan to live.

Chemical Fertilizers

Living near a golf course sounds ideal for golfers but isn't necessary a healthy choice. An environment with lots of green space may sound appealing, but it doesn't necessarily translate into clean air. Why? Maintaining that lush, carpet-like green grass requires fertilization, and there is no guarantee that the ingredients in the fertilizer are organic, biodegradable and free of any health risks with prolonged exposure. The people spreading the fertilizer know this and use protective masks. Here's an example of a warning on one fertilizer box: "When applying the fertilizer wear goggles, a dust mask, long pants, a long-sleeve shirt and rubber boots. Keep people and pets off the grass for at least 24 hours after the application or until the lawn is dry. Do not apply on a windy day." After the fertilizer is applied on the grass, the wind carries small particles far beyond the golf course boundaries. Ground water is also affected. The rain washes out the fertilizer, which enters the ground water. This could affect the water quality in the area if the golf course is near a water treatment system or water is being extracted from wells in the area.

In various studies, (http://www.pmac.net/pesticides_fertilizers.html) the chemicals used in these fertilizers have been associated with negative effects on health and normal child development. Experiments performed by various research groups suggest that fertilizer mixtures can affect developing neurological, endocrine and immune systems, so children and developing fetuses are most at risk. If you truly desire to live near a golf course, it would be prudent to start investigating what practices are being employed in maintaining the golf course. If you would like more information on this subject, search the Internet by using these key words: "fertilizers health," "fertilizer problems."

Recycling

Many counties in the world recognize the need to reduce our "footprint" on the environment and have implemented programs and initiatives to make environmental protection a priority. Both private and governmental entities have developed guidelines and programs promoting recycling (see articles in the Environmental Leader http://www.environmentalleader.com/.) "Sustainable development" (see http://www.iisd.org/ for more details) has come to the forefront of many organizations. Massive initiatives have been financed to develop methods that deal with recyclable materials (search the Internet for "recycling programs.") Factories have been built to process the materials and place them back in the manufacturing cycle. The population is expected to sort recyclable materials in color-coded bins, which are collected regularly from houses and buildings.

As a new member in your community you can play an active role in protecting and preserving the environment. The onus is on you to become informed and act in a responsible manner alongside other citizens in your community. Learn about the recycling program in your community. Call the city information line (or talk to your landlord) to find out pickup days and times. Properly sort and place recyclables in the designated containers. Glass and metals are separated from paper, cardboard and plastics and non-recyclable garbage is disposed of in separate bags, properly sealed. Tree branches, leaves and soil are also collected in a separate bag. Some people engage in composting, whereby organic waste is turned into rich soil called humus, which can be used as a natural fertilizer for the garden.

Recycling programs have been expanded to include appliances, TV sets, personal computers and other devices built with electric components (electrical or electronic device.) These items, also known as "electronic waste" or "e-waste," must be properly recycled, as they often contain harmful chemicals or precious metals that should not end up in a landfill. Many computer and electronics companies have developed programs whereby end-of-life or defective products are returned to them for recycling, so be sure to check with the manufacturer before you dispose of any electronic device.

Environmental awareness is also linked to the very popular "carbon footprint." This subject is well documented on the web. In short, it means that everything we consume corresponds to an amount of carbon released into the air. The gas and electricity we consume link either directly or indirectly to carbon emissions that affect the air quality and climate change. If the electricity comes from a plant that burns coal to produce electricity, every watt of power you consume is equivalent to a quantity of carbon dioxide (CO_2) that is released into the atmosphere. The car you drive and the bus or plane you take burn gas in order to run, which emits a quantity of CO_2 into the atmosphere. Riding your bike whenever possible will eliminate these emissions, as well as help you stay in shape. Carefully planning and optimizing your car or bus trips around the city will make you an active participant in the environmental protection program.

In conclusion, the less we consume and the more we recycle, the better we protect and preserve the environment, which leads to better air quality and a safer, healthier environment. If we take care of nature, nature will take care of us. Whenever possible, purchase recycled products instead of new ones. Instead of throwing items away, try to fix them. By recycling these products, you keep them away from our landfills. The more items you reuse, the less you'll need to purchase, which results in a reduced demand for these items. When the demand is low, manufacturers produce less, thereby using less of the earth's resources. As technology improves, manufacturing efficiency will increase and fewer resources will be used to manufacture products. All of this will help to lower our carbon footprint. To learn about other ways you can protect the environment and support sustainability, search the Internet for "how to protect environment."

XII. 3 Food

Industrialization of the food industry has increased productivity and has resulted in a large variety of products at affordable prices. As the industrialization revolution progressed, chemistry became very instrumental in the development of new products and tastes. Artificial flavors and colors have now replaced natural ingredients in many of the products on supermarket shelves. Globalization has created new opportunities for the food producers but requires that products be kept fresh for a longer period of time. It is safe to say that all the products we eat these days have been touched in one way or another by the industrial revolution and that they contain at least one chemical substance—either inside or sprayed on them—to keep them fresh and free of bacteria.

Nowadays, most new products are developed in a laboratory and contain chemicals. Each country supposedly has regulatory bodies that test and approve food products for commercialization. The question is, how long do they test these food products and what kinds of tests do they run? Years from now, someone may develop a certain disposition but would never be able to associate it with a specific food product because we have such a varied diet. So what do we do to protect ourselves? We take preventive measures. We become proactive. Most packages sold in the western world list the ingredients. Make a point of reading the list of ingredients on all packaged products you buy. Try to avoid products that contain artificial ingredients, including coloring and flavoring. Find out if they contain any other chemicals that might have a negative effect on your overall health and then decide for yourself if it is really what you want to eat. There is no known link between taste and nutrition value. In other words if it is tasty does not mean it is also full of the nutrients that one needs. In fact there are foods that do not taste great but are loaded with nutrients. A tasty product will make you eat more of it and even want some more once you finished it, but this does not mean it is also feeding you the right nutrients.

The industrial food industry doesn't just make new products; it also genetically modifies existing ones so they appear bigger and more beautiful. Commonplace in grocery stores are giant fruits and vegetables—apples, plums, peaches, seedless grapes and watermelons, to name only a few. Apart from their size and appearance, you may also notice that the taste is not the same. In some cases, produce has been genetically engineered to increase in size at the expense of taste. In other cases, the soil in which the product grows doesn't support such crops, which affects the taste.

The industry has also found ways to increase the productivity of animals and birds. Cows, pigs and chickens are fed genetically modified foods that are sometimes augmented with synthetic methionine, one of the essential amino acids in swine and poultry nutrition. Improper conversion of methionine can lead to atherosclerosis. (See http://en.wikipedia. org/wiki/Methionine. More information on genetically modified crops for poultry and livestock production is available at http://www.eaap.org/docs/GMOs_Antalya/GMOs_in_Antalya.

htm). In some cases, animals have been genetically modified in order to improve their performance (more meat, milk, eggs) which then become raw materials for products like cheese and precooked, ready-to-eat foods that may contain additional chemicals and taste-enhancers. (For more information on the research and development work being done in the genetics field, visit http://www.genesdiffusion.com/ and http://www. newsham.com.) Like genetically modified fruits and vegetables, this food is subjected to rigorous inspection and deemed to contain no substances known to have a negative effect on people's health. The point here is that you are still ingesting products that have been genetically modified and/or chemically engineered and treated to make it safe for consumption, *based on our present knowledge of what's safe.* Of course, this doesn't mean that they couldn't potentially harm us in the long run. Some people are not comfortable eating genetically modified and/or chemically engineered products while others are not concerned at all. Only you can decide which category you fit in.

On a lighter note, if you're hoping to find all the food products you're used to when shopping for food, think again. There's a good chance you'll see many unfamiliar products on grocery store shelves. Until you become accustomed to the new packaging and boxes, read the labels carefully to ensure you are buying items you actually want. Remember that colorful, attractive packages do not always contain healthy, nutritious products. Read the list of ingredients and nutrition information.

Organic products are becoming increasingly popular these days, but they can cost 30% to 50% higher than similar non-organic products. It's a good idea to check with the certifying authority in your area to determine exactly what "organic" means, as this can vary from place to place. A certification stamp generally means that a set of prerequisites has been met for manufacturing the product. These requirements vary from country to country and even between certifying authorities within territorial jurisdiction in the same country.

"Natural" products usually have a higher price tag than products containing chemicals. (For example, a "free-range" chicken is more expensive than a regular chicken.) This is because natural products are normally manufactured by small, family-owned businesses with production volumes that are lower than those of large national and multinational companies. In many cities, however, there are farmers' markets, where you can purchase natural products at more reasonable prices.

XII. 4 Safety

The crime rate is the indicator that best defines the safety of a community. You can obtain crime rate information from your local police station or police headquarters. Find out how your community compares with other neighborhoods. Look for tips published by the police department on how to maintain a safe community. Participate in activities that help to reduce the crime rate.

Contact Social Services to find out how your government assists the poor and disadvantaged. This information will give you an insight into how the system works and what kind of support is being offered to the people who need it. If the system is not providing them with adequate support, they will desperately look for a way to survive. In the process, they may operate outside the law and/or commit crimes against fellow citizens. While collecting this information, familiarize yourself with the rules regarding unemployment benefits, as they will come in handy should you become unemployed in future.

CHAPTER XIII.

INVESTING YOUR MONEY

MANAGING YOUR PERSONAL finances and reaching your financial goals can take a considerable amount of time and effort. Optimizing expenses to increase savings allows you to do more with your income. However, once you have reached your savings goals do not stop there. While the savings accumulate in your account you need to give consideration to certain factors that affect the value of money. Among them we can find the inflation and currency volatility. Because investing can be complicated, many people hire a financial planner or advisor to help them manage their investments and achieve their long-term financial goals. Paying a financial planner to manage your finances may make sense if you are a business owner or have multiple sources of revenue, tax-sheltered or long-term investments, and/or childcare expenses. Some people hire financial advisors because it frees them up for more important activities. It will be up to you to determine whether or not the time you save and the money you earn on your investments are worth the commission you pay your advisor for his or her services. This commission may be in the form of a percentage of the amount you invest, a flat fee, hourly fee, or a percentage of your assets or income. I recommend you ask your planner if he or she receives any benefit other than commission. (The questions to ask a planner before hiring him or her are outlined at http://www.fpsc-canada.org/public/articles/10_questions_ask_your_planner.) For privacy reasons, I also suggest that your advisor manage only your investment portfolio and not your entire finances. He or she will develop an investor profile containing your preferences in terms of investing money at a certain point in time, and nothing about you as an individual.

In this chapter I will discuss some of the ways in which you can invest your funds. Savings accounts, bonds, guaranteed investment certificates (GICs) involve little or no risk, whereas mutual funds and stocks come with more risk. I will also explain how currency volatility can affect the value of your money. Lastly, I will outline the best methods for transferring money to your friends and family overseas.

Keep in mind that your investment options are not limited to just the ones I discuss here. Other choices include investing in foreign currency, precious metals, real estate or a business (yours or someone else's). I recommend you investigate all the investment options available to you.

XIII. 1 Savings Accounts, GICs and Bonds

People often open separate savings accounts for specific purposes such as vacations, their children's education, professional development, car repairs or upgrades, aid for family abroad, etc. Bank savings accounts earn low interest but are a safe, secure vehicle for your money. In order to earn interest at the highest interest rate, you may have to deposit a large amount of money ($5,000 or more). Also, it is difficult to find a savings account with an interest rate high enough to at least equal the inflation rate. The value of money depreci-ates or decreases over time due to inflation. (If inflation last year was, say, 3%, this means it will cost $103 to purchase the same basket of products you paid $100 last year.) If pos-sible, we want to make up the loss due to inflation, not only to save money but also to preserve its value over time. In order to increase the value of your money with at least 3% per year (using the inflation rate in this example), you will need to in-vest it in something other than a savings account. Normally, the interest paid by the banks in North America doesn't cover the inflation rate unless the deposited amount is considerably high. To earn returns greater than the inflation rate, you must choose the next safe investment option: government-issued bonds or guaranteed investment certificates (GICs). Visit your local bank advisor to discuss the rates and terms for the spe-cific products they offer (Note: these vary from bank to bank). If you wish, review your options with your financial advisor before you make a final decision.

XIII. 2 Mutual Funds

If you are comfortable with a certain amount of risk, consider investing in mutual funds. The first step you should take be-fore you actually invest is to build your investor profile. Your investor profile will tell you what volatility level you can com-fortably tolerate. Your bank should be able to help with this. If not, you can easily find the information you need to build one on your own on the Internet. Use the search words "investor profile" then select the funds that fall within the acceptable limits of your investor profile in terms of *volatility* and *rate of return*. In building your investor profile, you will also establish the *timeframe* for your investment. For example, some funds may provide great returns on a short term (one to three years) and then fall under your desired minimum return. Others may provide lower returns in the early years but handsome gains in the long run (five to ten years).

In order to find the right mutual fund(s) for you, do some research on your own or talk to a financial advisor. (I don't recommend arbitrarily choosing a mutual fund in which to invest your life savings.) You should be able to easily obtain reports on each mutual fund on your bank's website or in printed format at your local branch. Each mutual fund should indicate, among other things, the *volatility* rating and *rate of return*. Volatility most frequently refers to "the standard deviation of the change in value of a financial instrument with a specific time horizon." This simply means that the change in fund value is frequent and extreme when the volatility is high and vice versa. The "change in value" can be positive or negative. Select only funds that are within the acceptable volatility level based on your investor profile. Eliminate those funds that provide returns lower than your acceptable level based on your desired return on investment within a given timeframe.

Other factors also come into play, depending on each fund's portfolio distribution. A mutual fund may hold investments in multiple companies across multiple industries. Factors that can affect a fund's evolution over time include but are not limited to market stability, economic situation, fund management, employment data, manufacturing sector strength, political events, and even the weather. Predicting a fund's evolution over time is difficult. Each analyst will retrieve the data and interpret it his or her own way, which results in a broad range of opinions on how the fund value will evolve. This is why talking to a financial advisor about the price evolution of a fund and which fund to choose among a pool of, say, ten funds that meet your criteria will only give you one person's opinion. Talking to a second and third advisor will most likely result in three different opinions. I also recommend that you do some research on your own—the more information you have, the better!

XIII. 3 The Stock Market

As you may have heard, investing in the stock market is not for everyone. The options are endless, so it's important that you have a good knowledge of the industry you choose to invest in and that you are prepared to lose money in the beginning. Considering the number of factors that can affect each individual stock evolution, it's anyone's guess which way the shares value in each stock will go. Even the most skilled futures analysts are taken by surprise sometimes. This is one subject that cannot be covered in one book and requires serious study in order to achieve good returns. If possible, take some financial investing courses, read books on the subject, and research the Internet using the search words "how to trade stocks."

XIII. 4 Currency Volatility

At least once in our lives we experience a variance in the currency value. This variance usually means our currency loses value and we pay more for the same product. This loss in value can seriously affect your savings if it is all in the same currency. The currency may also lose value on international markets, where more units are needed to purchase the currency of another country. This can seriously impact the economy of a country, particularly if it imports or exports goods and services to other countries.

It is good practice to distribute your savings across a wide range of investment options to reduce the exposure to high loss risk, especially if your purpose for saving money is to allow you to reach some of your long-term goals—retirement, your children's education, etc. When the currency you are using loses value, it becomes more difficult to attain these goals. Because of this, it is imperative that you not only take inflation into consideration but also the volatility risk by either increasing your target earnings with an estimated percentage (this percentage value varies, depending on the country and global economy) or purchase financial products that are more resilient to currency volatility. Instead of keeping the money in a savings account you could purchase bonds, mutual funds, stocks, etc., as discussed in the previous section. Another option is to purchase the more stable currency of another country. (Note: holding savings in another currency will alleviate to some degree the volatility issue but will not protect you from inflation.) One of the most preferred currencies at the end of the 20th century was the U.S. dollar. In recent days, however, the currency adopted by the European community, the Euro, has become the better option, having more stability and protection against volatility than the U.S. dollar.

Still another option is to place a portion of your savings or "safety net" in a universal currency such as gold (http:// en.wikipedia.org/wiki/Gold_as_an_investment). It is historically proven that at times of economical depression, the value of gold increases and at times of economical stability and progress it flattens or decreases. Investing in gold is particularly desirable when interest rates are low, in times of war and stagflation (search the Internet for definition), and during national crises. Gold is accepted throughout the globe and can be exchanged at global posted rates, regardless of the country. The percentage of your savings that you invest in gold will depend upon the political and economic environment of the country and the global market situation. For example, it may be worth placing a higher percentage (20% to 30 %) of your savings in gold at the beginning of a period of economical instability or at the first sign of a recession. Then, at the end of the unstable period, you could rebalance your portfolio by reducing the amount invested in gold and increasing the amount invested in other financial products that look promising at that time.

XIII. 5 Sending Money and Goods to Family and Friends

It is common for people working abroad to provide financial support to their family and friends in their country of origin. When it comes to sending money or goods abroad, you have several options. For example, you can send a check, money order or bank draft to the recipient via courier or postal service. In most of the cases, the bank is able to process the document only if the receiver holds an account at that bank. Of course, the simplest, safest and most cost-effective way of sending money or goods is by asking a friend or relative to act as courier. In this case, you must let them know all the restrictions related to what you are sending. It would be unfortunate if your friends ran into problems at the border because of the contents of your parcel or the amount of money they were carrying. Since many countries request that travelers crossing their borders report amounts of money over a certain limit ($10,000, for example), the onus is on you to verify the amount that your friends or relatives are transporting on your behalf.

Another way to send money is through your local bank branch. Although this method is safe, it can be complex. Your bank will charge you a fee for wiring the money to the recipient's bank account, which must be at a bank that accepts international wire transfers. Bank wire transfers are cost effective for large sums of money and if the sending and receiving banks are members of the same banking group or in partnership. Should you decide to send the money this way, you will need to get details about the receiver's bank, including the Bank Identifier Code (BIC) or SWIFT Code and the receiver's account number at that bank. This kind of transfer can take hours or even days to complete.

You may also transfer money via MoneyGram or Western Union. You will find other methods by searching the Internet for "international money transfer," all of which charge a fee. This fee can be a flat fee or based on the amount transferred. Each of these services comes with various restrictions and conditions. Before you attempt to send money overseas, make sure the service provider you have chosen operates in the city where the recipient resides. He or she will pick up the money at one of the service provider's locations, after providing proper identification, etc. Ensure the receiver can produce such documentation/information at the receiving end.

Many people send and receive money using PayPal. In this case, both the receiver and the sender must create online accounts at www.paypal.com. Money may be transferred from the sender's account to the receiver's account. Transferring money from Paypal into a bank account is only possible when the account has been "verified." After money is transferred into the receiver's account, it can be used for purchasing goods or services directly from on-line stores and companies that accept PayPal, or transferred into a bank account. (At the time of writing, money transfers from PayPal to a bank account are possible in only a limited number of countries.)

In terms of quality of service, take into account not only the fees but also the time required to transfer the money. Some providers might charge low fees but it may take longer for the money to arrive at the destination. Make sure the transaction is secure and that the service provider is not collecting too much of your personal information. Even if it is a large, well-established company, you should challenge the necessity of collecting information such as your date of birth, social insurance number, or bank account access (PIN).

If you choose to send goods to your loved ones, I recommend you first look into using the local postal service before a local or global courier (UPS, FedEx) because the local postal and courier service fees will be lower. (I do not recommend using a courier or postal service to send money.) Your first step should be to call the service providers or visit their websites to find out how to use their service. Each provider will explain in detail the procedure, provide a list of locations and outline the fees charged for their service. Be sure to inquire about the pickup and delivery schedules and times for each type of service. If the procedures seem cumbersome, rest assured this is to ensure the security of the transaction for all parties—the company offering the service, you, and the receiver. Secondly, find out if there are restrictions for sending certain products out of the country. (You can obtain a list of restrictions from the Customs or Border Control agency.) The goods sent abroad are being "exported" from the country of origin and "imported" at destination, so you'll want to know what, if any, import fees will be charged at the destination. (Note: imported goods exempt from taxes may still be subject to an inspecting/processing fee.) If the customs fees are too high for the receiver to pay, it may be better to send money instead of the item.

CHAPTER XIV.

ENJOYING LIFE

OUR FAST-PACED LIFESTYLE can sometimes make it difficult to us to balance work, play, exercise and family life. In this chapter I discuss the benefits of establishing a fitness program as well as some of the ways to enjoy your leisure time. As the saying goes, *Mens sana in corpore sano* (a healthy mind in a healthy body)!

XIV. 1 Staying Fit

Before beginning any fitness program, I suggest you have a doctor assess your condition and confirm that you are healthy enough to do so. Keep in mind that not all the advertised workout routines will be suitable for your body. Make sure you are getting enough sleep and are well rested. Nutrition is very important, so make sure you are eating healthy foods that will give you the energy you need. You will get the best results when your body is ready to exercise. To maintain optimum energy, you may need to consult with a nutritionist. Alternatively, you can learn about nutrition by searching the Internet using the words "fitness and nutrition." It has been scientifically demonstrated that keeping your body in good condition through exercise, proper nutrition and sleep will extend your life expectancy. Once you receive the go-ahead from your doctor, you are ready to develop an exercise routine. Many people prefer to hire a personal trainer to work with them, but this isn't necessary. (Look up "workout plan" on the Internet and choose one that you believe you can handle, or visit http://www.in-motion.ca/walkingworkout/plan/.) Your trainer and nutritionist can monitor your progress over time and work with you to achieve your fitness goals.

Your workout plan doesn't have to be complicated or expensive. All you need is three or four exercise routines twice a week that will raise your heart rate to the appropriate level and strengthen and tone your muscles. Your options might include working out on machines at home or at a gym (strength training), or a combination of strength training and walking, jogging, swimming or other sports activities (cardiovascular training). Improve your upper body strength using a chin-up/pull-up bar. Strengthen your core plus upper and lower body with an "exercise wheel". The more varied the exercises, the better. (Of course, you should always avoid sports that could aggravate a medical condition.) Consider purchasing ad-hoc or monthly/yearly passes at your local gym, or look for gym equipment that you can use at home. (Depending on how often you exercise, it may be more cost- effective to buy your own equipment.) Whenever possible, exercise outdoors in the fresh air. Look for opportunities to jog outdoors rather than on a treadmill. Some parks in your area may have bike paths. Find a circuit of about 10 km and use it at least once per week. Bike to work, join a soccer, tennis, racquetball or squash club or try out the country's national sport with your friends.

XIV. 2 Keeping Entertained

Leisure time plays an integral part in achieving life-work balance. Your life plan includes many activities that fall into the "work" category, so it's crucial that you schedule time for "play" activities that energize you, make you happy, and that will recharge your batteries so you can continue to be fully engaged in life. In today's world there are endless ways to have a good time or relax. All it takes is a little bit of imagination and some planning.

Spending time with friends, watching TV and listening to music are popular ways to ease everyday stresses and strains. Many people enjoy movies, live theatre, opera or concerts while others prefer to hit golf balls at the driving range or visit a museum. (Don't forget to research the budget cinemas in your area.) Still others find it relaxing to shop, stroll through the park, meditate or visit a spa. Craft projects are very attractive to many; a wide variety of free project ideas are available online. Camping outdoors with friends or family will give you a break from today's fast-paced environment (get completely un-plugged). For more adventurous types there is river rafting, mountain climbing or hikes through tropical forests or jungles. For non-adventurous types there are vacation packages to beach resorts where you can enjoy your favorite drink while sunbathing and listening to the waves, or cruises where you can visit exotic places while enjoying the convenience of shops, restaurants, casinos, and pools on huge ships or "floating hotels."

If you would rather stay close to home, or if time is limited, contact the visitor's centre in your town or city and go to some of the places they recommend. If you have a bit more time, target historical sites, fairs, expositions, science or aviation museums, or other popular tourist attractions. If you run out of ideas, visit the local library or a bookstore and look under the tourism sections. As always, the Internet is an endless source of inspiration. Start your search by simply looking for "things to do in <your region>" or "sights and attractions <your region>." (You could also replace <your region> with <your city> in your search.)

If you want to have some family fun with your children, take them to a playground, a fun house, a corn maze or a place where they can ride go-karts (miniature cars). If you prefer to stay home, rent a movie at your local video store or play a board game (search the Internet for "board games" or "family board games"). Board games are fun for people of all ages.

CHAPTER XV.

FINAL STEPS

CONGRATULATIONS ON MAKING it this far! The road may have been long and bumpy, but you managed to achieve your goals and make your dream a reality. None of this would have been possible without clear vision, determination, perseverance, patience and good decision-making. What you've accomplished is nothing short of outstanding. Because of your efforts, the future looks very bright for you and your loved ones.

Let's recap what you've gone though to complete the great immigration adventure:

- ✓ Made one of the biggest decisions in a lifetime (thinking, analyzing, options weighting)
- ✓ Researched and planned for the move
- ✓ Learned how to gather the money required to immigrate
- ✓ Became very familiar with living costs (transportation, housing, etc.) in a new country

✓ Took a job-hunting crash course and discovered the challenges of finding good employment
✓ Learned about the importance of social and community integration
✓ Read about the language and cultural barrier
✓ Read about nationalism and multiculturalism in the context of immigration
✓ Learned about nutrition and ways to identify healthy foods
✓ Learned about the invisible elements that affect our health
✓ Learned about the insurance (social, health, auto and home) and education systems
✓ Learned more about taxation and the banking system
✓ Read about money saving and decision-making strategies
✓ Learned about investing your savings
✓ Learned about protecting the environment and how to get involved
✓ And finally, found ways to keep entertained and active

XV. 1 Becoming a Citizen

People who choose to emigrate from their native land in search of a better place for their family will follow a process similar to the one I have described in this book. The last step of this process, the final stop in the immigration journey, is obtaining your citizenship. Obtaining citizenship does not negate your origin or aspects of your unique identity—your culture, religion, race or mother tongue—but it does give you what you wanted so badly and worked so hard for: the same rights, privileges and responsibilities as all other citizens of your adopted country.

It may be mandatory for you to surrender your existing citizenship before being eligible to obtain citizenship in your adoptive country. I suggest you determine the requirements for becoming a citizen early on in the immigration process, ideally prior to engaging in it. I also recommend you find out how to regain the citizenship of your country of origin in case this should become necessary or desirable. If you choose not to surrender your citizenship, you will maintain your "permanent resident" status. In most cases, you will be allowed to maintain "dual citizenship," but this has some implications. For more information on this, search the Internet using the search words "dual citizenship." (At the time of writing, an in-depth article on this topic was available at http://www.cic.gc.ca/english/resources/publications/dual-citizenship.asp.)

The process of obtaining citizenship varies from country to country, but you will always need to personally request it. You can apply for citizenship only after you have obtained permanent residence status and met certain eligibility criteria. (Note: some people choose not to apply for citizenship and instead maintain their permanent resident status, where they have limited rights and privileges. This decision can involve extra effort in maintaining the conditions of permanent residency status.) After a waiting period, you fill out an application form, attach supporting documentation and submit it for processing. Sometimes applications are accepted via the Internet, but given the need for supporting documentation the applications are usually mailed. A regulatory body will process the application and verify all the supporting documents. This process also takes time, usually several months. (In fact, the entire immigration process, including the wait time prior to being allowed to immigrate, plus the permanent residence period—the time you spend in the adoptive country until you are eligible to become a citizen—could easily stretch over five years.) During this time, communication with the ministry will take place via mail. The citizenship application processing office may request additional information or action on your part. They will also notify you of the date of the citizenship ceremony and/or other final steps in the process. Try to keep the same address as the one recorded on your application. If you do move, inform the processing office and request confirmation that the change was recorded. Notify the post office of your change of address to ensure your mail is redirected.

XV. 2 Applying for a Passport

Once you have obtained citizenship, you may want to apply for a passport reflecting your new status. A passport gives you the freedom to travel abroad as a citizen of your adoptive country. Access to countries you always wanted to visit may have just become a whole lot easier. While traveling with your new passport, you may be able to enter some countries without a visitor's visa. (Mutual agreements between your adoptive country and the country you visit may have waived the requirement for entry visas.) Keep in mind, however, that you may still need to obtain a visa if you are planning to work abroad. Also, your new citizenship status may have changed your eligibility to enter or remain in some countries.

To obtain a passport you must first go through the application process. Learn about the process specific to your new country by searching the Internet for "passport application process <country>." Application forms are generally available at postal outlets, passport offices or on the Internet, along with instructions on the application process and the required documentation. After you have filled out the application form and had your photo taken (at a designated photo studio or shop), you may apply in person at the passport office. (If you live in a major city, you will likely find it convenient to visit the local passport office. You may be given the option to apply for a passport by mail, but there are risks in sending away all of your original documents. In this case, you must also include a self-addressed, prepaid envelope so the office can mail your documents back to you.) Because passport offices are usually busy, I suggest you find out what hours they are open and the typical wait times. After you have shown your original documents to an officer, he or she will verify your identity and eligibility, make copies of your documents and return them to you, and then ask you to pay a fee or provide proof of payment (this varies from country to country).

If you applied in person, it normally takes about ten business days for your new passport to be returned to you. (If you would like it sooner, additional fees apply.) If you applied by mail, your passport will be mailed back to you, along with your original documents, in about four weeks. To determine the processing time for passports issued in your new country, search the Internet for "processing times passport <country>."

Closing Note

I HOPE YOU found the contents of this book useful and informative. My intention in sharing this information was to make it easier for you to deal with the many issues you will face in the immigration process. It is my hope that the knowledge I passed on in this book will help you find your way so you can spend more time with your family or simply enjoy life.

I wish you much success and happiness on your journey.

If you wish to share your opinion or comment about this book, please visit www.theimmbook.org

List of Internet Links

I. 2 Gathering Information
http://www.travail-solidarite.gouv.fr/informations-pratiques/
fiches-pratiques/duree-du-travail/duree-legale-du-travail.html
http://www.travail-solidarite.gouv.fr/foire-aux-questions/con-
ges-payes.html
http://www.canadaone.com/ezine/july07/vacation.html
http://www.cbc.ca/news/interactives/map-vacation-days/

II. 1 The Immigration Process
http://www.cic.gc.ca/
http://www.uscis.gov/

II. 3 Making Plans
http://www.cbp.gov/xp/cgov/travel/vacation/kbyg/prohibited_
restricted.xml
http://www.customs.gov.au/site/page.cfm?u=4369
http://www.cbsa-asfc.gc.ca/publications/pub/rc4151-eng.html

III. 3 Travel by Air, Step by Step
http://en.wikipedia.org/wiki/Boarding_pass

X. 3 Public Transportation
http://www.vtpi.org/tca/tca0502.pdf

X. 4 Biking: the Environmental Choice
http://www.kenkifer.com/bikepages/advocacy/autocost.htm

XI. 1 Urban vs. Suburban Living
http://www.ceosforcities.org/

XI. 2 Renting vs. Buying a Home
https://ssl.postescanada-canadapost.ca/smartmoves/check-list/default-e.aspx
http://www.scribd.com/doc/3675696/US-National-Association-of-Realtor-Statistics-19682008-Annual-Home-Appreciation-based-on-the-median-price-of-homes-sold-62508
http://www.free-books.us/us_national_association_of_realtor_statistics_1968_2008_median_price_on_home_sales_6_25_08.php&free_ebook=3675699
http://www.ourfamilyplace.com/homebuyer/first.html

XI. 3 Selling your Home
http://www.bls.gov/k12/money05.htm

XII. 2 Environmental Issues
http://www.mercola.com/article/emf/emf_dangers.htm
http://www.emfacts.com/papers/cfs.html
http://www.feb.se/ARTICLES/electrosmog.html
http://energy.cr.usgs.gov/radon/georadon/2.html
http://www.pmac.net/pesticides_fertilizers.html
http://www.environmentalleader.com/
http://www.iisd.org/

XII. 3 Food
http://en.wikipedia.org/wiki/Methionine
http://www.eaap.org/docs/GMOs_Antalya/GMOs_in_Antalya.

htm
http://www.genesdiffusion.com/
http://www.newsham.com

XIII. Investing Your Money
http://www.fpsccanada.org/public/
articles/10_questions_ask_your_planner

XIII. 4 Currency Volatility
http://en.wikipedia.org/wiki/Gold_as_an_investment

XIII. 5 Sending Money and Goods to Family and Friends
www.paypal.com

XIV. 1 Staying Fit
http://www.in-motion.ca/walkingworkout/plan/

XV. 1 Becoming a Citizen
http://www.cic.gc.ca/english/resources/publications/dual-citi-zenship.asp

About The Author

ANDY STORM IS a project manager and writer best known for his persuasiveness, ambition and ability to get things done. He was born and raised in Bucharest, the capital city of Romania. Early on, he became fascinated by how things work and loved to relate stories about what he learned to friends and family.

Andy is considered by some to be an autodidact, or "self-educator." After completing his Master's degree in Computer Science, Andy decided to apply his knowledge to the IT industry and make plans for the future. In 2001, he decided to immigrate to Canada. According to Andy, this is when his real life education took place. The knowledge, experience and lessons learned during his immigration adventure and journeys throughout Europe and North America are reflected in *Open Borders*.

Andy currently lives with his family in Ottawa, Canada and is working on his next book entitled *10 Percent Fiction*, a series of short stories describing life in communist '80s and post-communist '90s society.